CLIMBING CLOUDS
CATCHING COMETS

Poems by
ALEXANDER "KING" PAUL

Biography by
JOANNA BROWN

Poetry

First Printed in United Kingdom 2018

Published by Conscious Dreams Publishing
www.consciousdreamspublishing.com

Edited by Lee Caleca

Typeset by Nadia Vitushynska

ISBN: 978-1-912551-23-1

Dedications

To everyone who knew and loved Alexander "King" Paul.

Acknowledgements

Thank you God for giving me the strength and courage to compile this book during the sad and most difficult time of my life. Thank you for allowing me the privilege to be the mother of Alexander Maurice Paul.

Thanks to Alexander for leaving this legacy of poems behind that enabled me to throw myself into such a project and feel as if I was almost as talented and gifted as he was.

The two most important people who helped to prepare this book are Melanie Anning and Siana Bangura.

Melanie edited my narratives, producing concise and eloquent wording to my expressed recollections of Alexander's life.

Siana acted as my agent and advisor providing me with all the knowledge she gained as a self-published author writing the poetry book *Elephant*.

Thank you so much to Tunde Bolaji for designing the background to the book cover and to Daniella Blechner, Founder of Conscious Dreams Publishing, who provided a partnership service to get this book published.

Thank you Nick Timothy for taking an interest in my son and giving him a marvellous opportunity to shine. It was only fitting to ask you to write the foreword which I truly appreciate.

I thank my family in particular: Lamarr, Sharon, Pauline and Christine for giving love and support and being there during the difficult times as we grieved for the loss of our loved one.

I am also extremely grateful to the regular visits and support form Alexander's many friends and those who have become part of my extended family; too many to mention personally. My daughters Shanika, Titi, Rochelle have all given me positive support. Thank you Sholape and Tunde and Rodney for being true to your promise that you would never leave us.

My besties, Beryl, Barbara and Jennifer have provided emotional and physical support with sound counselling at times.

I thank Chatsworth Baptist Church for providing me with spiritual and practical support and helping so much during the long illness. This church has provided a haven for me to run into and seek strength from the Lord when needed.

Thank you everyone else who have given me support over the last 20 months, loving me and my family and helping to produce this book. I'm sure we will all continue to work on other future projects continually inspired by our dear Alexander.

'Love and Blessings'

Foreword

I first met Alexander in April 2014. He came to the Home Office with some friends from his sixth form college to take part in a round-table discussion about their experiences of being stopped and searched by the police. In a group of bright young adults, Alexander's fierce intelligence stood out.

After the meeting, I wrote to each of the students who had given us their time, and Alexander and I stayed in touch. Learning about his keen interest in politics and the media, I offered to help by mentoring him and making introductions so he could get work placements.

As a result, Alexander spent time working with Sky News and, after I had left the Home Office, with Theresa May's team there. At Sky, he became friends with Afua Hirsch, the journalist and author. At the Home Office, he read his poem about being stopped and searched in front of Theresa and members of her private office. I know how deeply touched she was by his words.

Alexander was such an extraordinary talent, I believe he could have gone on to be a great success in whatever field he chose. It was easy to imagine him becoming a writer, a performer, a journalist, a politician, a human rights campaigner, or even a successful entrepreneur: I know about the commercial qualities he showed while he was at university! And he was a gifted footballer too.

My abiding memory of him, however, will always be the moment he introduced Theresa before her keynote speech at the Conservative Party Conference. Most people of his age would have been overawed, speaking in front of such a large audience, live on television, and introducing the Home Secretary. But if Alexander was nervous, he did not show it. Within seconds, it was clear he had struck up a rapport with the audience, but he did not simply say what they wanted to hear. He challenged their preconceptions, he made an argument, and I am sure he changed many people's minds that day.

Anybody who knew Alexander knew what a special young man he was. His death last year was a cruel blow not only to his mother, Joanna, but to all of us who were lucky enough to have him in our lives. We will never know the people he would have helped, the lives he would have touched, and the family he would have loved. But in this anthology of poetry, we will remember him, and remember his very rare talent.

Nick Timothy, Political Advisor

Contents

Introduction

"I pray that this book can be the impetus for you and your growth as a songwriter. Go and live the dream, do what you and I know feels right: Create. Do what you love, Mum.

With Love,
Alexander"

Those words were written in a book in January 2016. A book that would be the last birthday gift my son would ever give me.

Alexander had taken action after hearing me speak constantly about my dream of becoming a songwriter. He kept encouraging me to follow through, reminding me that I was not too old to start and that there was no better time than the present. That was the kind of person he was, always encouraging and inspiring people.

2016 had started off well and I really believed it would be my year to achieve goals. However, on Friday 18th March, I received a call from one of Alexander's university friends informing me that he was in hospital and about to be placed in an induced coma after a series of uncontrollable seizures.

After an initial diagnosis of meningitis came the awful confirmation that Alex had an incurable cancerous growth on his brain.

Song writing went on the back burner and, eighteen months later, my desire to compose has been channelled into the process of preparing an Anthology of Alexander's poetry.

I have divided the book into two parts; the first consisting of small chapters containing narratives of the various stages in Alexander's short life to provide a profile of the person behind the poems. I made this decision after reading a few of his earlier poems. However, as I undertook the arduous task of transcribing the multitude of poems that Alexander had handwritten, I realised that his writings were akin to keeping a personal diary in the form of poetry, making it easier for any reader to glean facets of his personality. This is demonstrated in the Anthology Part 2.

The poems are listed in chronological order to showcase his skill as a writer as he matured and grew intellectually. Alexander always said that he was not the best spoken-word poet, but his passion for the craft made up for any shortcomings. Some of his earlier works were redrafted in 2015 and incorporated into new and expanded material, making it easier for Alexander to present them in the format of spoken-word poetry acceptable for live performances. This can be seen in his masterpiece "I AM LOVE", an adaptation of an earlier writing titled "I AM".

Alexander dated most of his work, but those without exact dates are placed at the end of the year in which they were written. There is a noticeable lack of poems in the year 2013 due to Alexander's concentration on achieving the 'A' grades required to get into Warwick, his chosen University. He gave titles to approximately ninety percent of his work but for the few that he missed, I have chosen titles, which suit the context of the poem for consistency and completeness. Some of the later 2015/16 poems appear to be unfinished but I have included them nevertheless. Otherwise, I have left his work untouched with the original manuscripts safely filed away.

My son was a strong and extremely fit young man who had the world before him and had just begun the journey of becoming an established spoken word poet at the time he collapsed. He was following his passion. He took pride in his appearance and well-being, rarely indulging in extravagant living. So it was a shock for everyone when he was diagnosed with brain cancer. Due to his fit state, everyone believed he would eventually recover especially as he remained mentally strong with a positive attitude. This was not to be and Alexander left this world before he had the opportunity to fulfil many of his ambitions.

He wanted to publish his collection of poems with a view that they would touch people and help someone going through depression or mental health issues. He was passionate that writing poetry could help to generate an attitude of self-love, which would overcome negative and self-destructive feelings. Alexander himself had gone through a period of depression and, at times, was introspective and melancholy. He stated that his release during these private moments was to "put pen to paper" and write, as there was "more power in a pen than a sword".

He got involved with the Mental Health Society at Warwick University and assisted in some of their workshops where he read and acted out one of his poems. He also wanted to set up a charity/fund to help people (predominately young men) to express themselves through poetry, spoken word or other art forms as a way of releasing pent up emotions.

I feel privileged and honoured to have had such a gifted son who so many people found to be kind, inspiring and fun-loving. To honour him and to put an end to my procrastination, I embarked on the challenge of trying to fulfil some of Alexander's wishes. I painstakingly transcribed most of his poems onto the computer editing where necessary, although not much work was needed in this regard. The poems written in later university years were just taken from his laptop and electronic devices.

For weeks, I racked my brain for a title for the anthology. His last and most prominent piece of work, "I AM LOVE", a poem he performed at the Warwick Music Festival, had already received some interest on social media, so at first this was a strong contender. However, one day, when I turned over the back cover of one of his poetry books written in 2010, there staring at me was the title, "A Rainbow of Emotions." I thought Alexander had even done this part of the work for me until I discovered, just prior to seeking publishers, that a published poetry book with the same title already exists. I eventually settled on *CLIMBING CLOUDS; CATCHING COMETS* (I am Love), an alliteration of words taken from the poem "I AM LOVE", which I think shows that my son had the ability to rise above the clouds and reach for the stars.

His poems truly cover the vicissitudes of life including love, hate, sadness, depression, broken hearts, sensuality, family breakdown, cultural pride, police brutality and much more.

Alexander may not have personally encountered every single emotion or experience that was written about in his poems but he had an extraordinary ability to put himself inside someone else's shoes and take on their emotions, a skill that most successful poets possess. I was often moved to tears as I went through his work as his poems took me from the depths of despair to the heights of great expectations, giving me a greater appreciation for my life and making me feel that I too could change this world for the better.

I hope when you finish reading this book, you will understand why the Prime Minister, Theresa May, paid tribute to Alexander and described him as 'inspiring' in her keynote speech at the Conservative Party conference three months after his death. After the publicity which followed his namecheck, I decided to bring forward plans to publish his work. After voicing my intention, I was thrust into action, despite being on the bereavement roller coaster.

Alexander would have been so proud to see me using my creative skills, choosing on a daily basis to be more proactive and defeating my desire to procrastinate.

Maybe that song will get written in the not too distant future; perhaps it will be a tribute to my beloved son, Alexander 'King' Paul.

Joanna Brown

PART 1

SHORT BIOGRAPHY

Alexander

Early Years

Alexander was born on the 11th of October 1995 at Cardiff University hospital in Wales. His mother, Joanna — a lawyer — was of Jamaican heritage, and his father, Francilien — CEO of a charity — was from Haiti. Alexander was a big baby, almost 10 pounds, and he was born with a six pack. Two years later, his brother Lamarr joined him.

Alexander's many talents emerged early; he began reading at three and by five he was writing stories in a notebook on a daily basis. It was around this time that he developed a love for literacy reading both fiction and non-fiction books and composing poems. This was nurtured initially at St. Luke's Primary School and then at Elmwood Primary School where his talent for sport also became evident.

From the first poems, (in Part 2 of this book) it was evident that Alexander was a deeply compassionate young boy and a peacemaker. He would mediate when there was conflict between friends and he tried hard to make people happy. He became a playground ambassador and helped other children resolve their problems. Alexander was already developing the diplomatic skills he was to demonstrate throughout his short life.

He also developed a talent for showmanship at Stagecoach Performing Arts and at six-years-old was selected to perform in a Christmas show at Norwood Theatre. Around this time, he became an avid Michael Jackson fan. For his 7th birthday party he insisted on dressing up as his hero and doing the moonwalk.

All who knew Alexander can testify to his passion for music and his dance skills. Dancing was a big part of his early years and it helped him develop into a confident showman. He never shied away from reading in front of a church full of people and would engage in debates with grown-ups, holding his own intellectually. He was charismatic and charming.

Alexander was a gifted athlete and had a competitive spirit. He strived to excel in whatever he did. At Elmwood, he played basketball, football and competed in athletics. As football captain, he achieved both individual and team success. He would go on to play football for the county. On many cold mornings, his mother Joanna stood on the pitch side shouting encouragement to the team. Alexander found this embarrassing and later lovingly asked her to "leave the shouting and coaxing to the coach".

Through his love of reading, Alexander's vocabulary advanced beyond his years. His father encouraged him to learn ten new words each day and one of his favourite pastimes in the early years was reading the dictionary. He was an inquisitive child who asked lots of questions which his parents would endeavour to answer.

Like all young children, Alexander had a lot of confidence in his mother and in the early years believed that she knew everything. She had always encouraged her boys to engage in activities such as scrabble, chess, card games, and quizzes. However, one day he asked Joanna the answer to a difficult grammatical question. She did not know it and he took the initiative to research and resolve the issue himself. From that day, he never again asked for help with his work, preferring to figure things out for himself. This was the beginning of many bitter-sweet moments, bitter for Joanna as she watched her son's knowledge surpass her own in some areas but sweet, knowing and seeing her child constantly pushing himself intellectually.

When Alexander was ten, his parents separated.

Secondary School Years

Between 2007 and 2012, Alexander attended St Joseph's Catholic Boys School in Upper Norwood. There, he continued to develop his passion for poetry and literature and also began displaying a talent for spoken-word performance, an art that highlighted both his social and verbal skills. In Year 9, he was honoured to receive the *Jack Petchy Award* for being an Outstanding Student.

Alexander was shining in a range of sports. He still played football but he also developed a love for basketball and subsequently rugby, which was to be short-lived following a kick to the head. Aged 12, he was scouted by both Fulham and Chelsea football clubs.

For nine months, Alexander trained with Fulham's youth academy up to three times a week after school, sometimes not returning home until 10pm, with homework to complete. Prioritising his goal of going to university, Alexander told his mother that continuing to play football would ruin his chances of achieving a sound academic record. He left Fulham.

At school, English appeared to be his strongest subject and by the time he was 16 he had written a poem called "Freedom or Free Doom", of which he was very proud.

Alexander was developing his spirituality through regular attendance at Chatsworth Baptist Church where he made major contributions as part of the youth team. Alexander was a popular figure not just amongst his peers. He spoke confidently to the adults and regularly made valid and intelligent contributions in ethical and spiritual debates.

However, as he made friends with children of other faiths and spiritual outlooks, Alexander began to question Christianity. His identity as a young black male was emerging and he was being influenced by musicians such as Bob Marley, who helped him to explore the Rastafarian faith and black culture through music. He also began to read about many inspirational and political thinkers and activists and in the early teenage years discovered the teachings of Malcolm X.

Sadly, it was during the later years of secondary school that Alexander became more sensitive to his mortality and the frailty of life. His beloved grandmother, who had been a great support to him following the breakup of his parents' marriage, developed cancer and after battling for two years died in April 2011. Alexander was devastated by her illness and death.

It was around this period that his most prolific and deepest outpourings in poetry were written. Alexander went through a transcendental period of soul searching, which made him sensitive, emotional and on occasions paranoid. Some of the poems show a preoccupation with death and a fear of imminent harm. It is as if he had a premonition that his life span would not be long, so he had to make each day count. This preoccupation appears to have developed around the time his grandmother was diagnosed with cancer.

Alexander had been three when his maternal grandfather died and this early experience of death impacted on him. He had so many mannerisms of his late grandfather and was always told that he resembled him, which helped Alexander develop a strong affinity despite having just vague memories of his presence.

At the age of 16, signs of depression were evident but Alexander rejected his mother's offer of attending counselling sessions, stating that he had his own way of dealing with his sadness, which was by putting pen to paper.

Although the family was aware of his poetry, it was not until much later at university that the full extent of Alexander's writing became apparent and even then the full depths of his depression were not revealed until after his death.

Much of Alexander's work alludes to his despair, loneliness and feelings of being misunderstood, from which he gained release through writing.

It depicts a difficult and introspective period although, outwardly, Alexander had many friends and appeared to be enjoying life.

He was determined to do well academically and worked hard in his exams in order to get into the college of his choice — St Xavier's in Clapham. Alexander also developed his love of music acknowledging that the talents of singers such as Marvin Gaye, Michael Jackson, Nina Simone, whom he would describe as troubled souls, greatly influenced his way of thinking and outlook on love and humanity. He studied music at GCSE level and played the bass guitar, aspiring at the time to play in a band like several of his maternal uncles.

Alexander, like most teenagers, became aware of his image and took pride in presenting himself as a well-dressed young man at all times, even at home. This came from his late grandmother who always told her grandchildren to stand tall and carry themselves proudly no matter how they were feeling.

His growing interest in the opposite sex and schoolboy crushes demonstrated that he was a passionate person who desired loved and gave generously of his emotions.

Alexander wrote most of his poems during this period of life. He was a teen having difficulties with his physical metamorphosis into an attractive young man and all the problems in dealing with emotions that adolescence throws up. He was a sensitive person who wanted good things for everyone he met but often took personal criticism or rejection so deeply that it, on occasions, affected his well-being. Despite these inward characteristics, they were rarely shown to the outside world who mainly saw Alexander as a team player, jovial, fun-loving, and certainly one for the ladies.

Stop and Search Years

Growing up in South London between Gipsy Hill and West Norwood was difficult for Alexander. He was a teenage black male being exposed to the streets or the 'hood' as young people referred to it.

He was an academic who pursued knowledge. From an early age he knew his own mind and what he wanted out of life. He was clean living, choosing not to smoke, he rarely drank alcohol and never took drugs.

Alexander was already tall and muscular in his early teenage years and appeared older than he was. So when he began to be stopped and searched around the age of 12-13 he was troubled by the attitude of some policemen.

Despite being advised by his mother — a lawyer — to note the police officers' personal numbers and politely inquire the reason for the search, Alex rarely did this, which made it difficult for Joanna to take matters further. At one stage after he and Lamarr had been stopped a few times in a short period, Joanna attended the local police station to find out why. However, without an identity number it was a wasted visit and only served to air her frustration at their unfair treatment.

Alexander and Lamarr occasionally played basketball and football in the 'cage' in the nearby council estate's playground. There Alexander would talk to many of the young people, some of whom had abandoned education and some who, like himself, saw it as a way forward. It was a time when a lot of young boys would gather on the streets as there was no youth club or community hall for them to hang out. Their presence attracted police attention and gave rise to frequent stop and searches. Although there may have been occasions when it was justified, this procedure was used disproportionately to target local young black boys and men.

On one occasion, Alexander was an hour late coming home from school and was not answering his mobile phone. When he finally arrived, he was in the foulest of moods, angry and distressed. Initially he refused to talk about what had happened. He said he had been put in a police van despite a negative stop and search procedure. His remonstrations of innocence were ignored. He was told that he fitted the description of a person who had stolen a mobile phone from a young boy. After being held for 40 minutes with no attempt to contact his parents, despite his age, the complainant arrived and immediately stated that he was not the person who had attacked him, as he was much taller. Alexander did not take the number of the police officers stating, "What's the point? Nothing would be done anyway."

Alexander shared another incident that occurred one day when he was coming home from college. He had been stopped by police who wrongly accused him of jumping over the train station barrier to avoid payment but were satisfied when they saw his travel card had been used and let him continue his journey. After that experience, Alexander came to the conclusion that he could no longer dress like an urban youth in tracksuits and trainers. The negative misconception was that a young black male dressed in a "hoodie" was likely to be a drug dealer/criminal.

His love of skinny jeans, jumpers and "nice shoes" had begun. Alexander was tired of the victimisation and stated that the powerful lesson learnt about diplomacy and compromise was worth it for an easier life. This period was just prior to changes of the 'stop and search' law.

He wrote a lot about experiences of police victimisation and, with poetic licence, life on the streets commencing around late 2010. He spoke about being an angry teenager, trying to find a place in this society. He had seen and heard about the many unpleasant things happening on the streets and chronicled the discrimination and brutality of this life. Alexander was also concerned for his younger brother.

Alexander found pride in his background and heritage despite the negative images put forward in the media and made it his duty to find out about black history and prominent people of African and Asian ancestry who had made contributions to society. Alexander believed that knowledge and education were the way forward in a society where black boys were seen as a nuisance and potential criminals.

It was against this background that Alexander was later pleased to be invited by Theresa May's team to discuss issues of 'stop and search' at the Home Office.

College Years

Alexander decided to pursue his 'A' Levels in a more relaxed, mixed environment and attended St Xavier's College, known as SFX, where he started out studying Politics, Religious Studies, English, and History.

There was early success. With the support of the English department, Alexander tidied up his early poem "Freedom or Free Doom" and it was published in *The Poetry Games (2013)*, an anthology of young poets *"who have created verse filled with passion, expression and, most importantly, their opinion on the subjects that matter most to them."* Alexander proudly boasted to his mother, "I told you I would be a published writer by the time I was 18."

In addition to studying hard, Alexander became a prolific poetry writer during his time at college. However, at the end of his first year, he dropped English after achieving a disappointing 'B' grade at 'AS' level. Despite his love for literacy, he wanted to be the best and he felt it was better to give up English, which was the most time consuming of his subjects, so that his other grades would not be impacted.

Alexander was determined to gain a place at Warwick University. He refused to consider Oxbridge, as he believed he would be unhappy there due to the lack of diversity. At this stage, he was greatly affected by what he perceived as the unequal treatment of black youths.

He was enjoying the freedom that college life brought and loved being in a mixed environment. He often moaned that he was sent to an all-boys senior school. Alexander loved female company and believed that women should be treated like the queens that they were. It was at college that his understanding of women's rights developed. Here too he met the love of his life — Shanika Wallace — when they both attended a sports trip to Czech Republic. He said that Shanika initially played 'hard to get' but, being an accomplished dancer herself, she was eventually won over by his famous moonwalk!

Their relationship was strong and respectful, with Shanika eventually gaining the title of 'Queen,' which Alexander had previously reserved for his mother. His love was now shared between two women who both meant the world to him for different reasons. Even going to university in Warwick did not dent their relationship as Shanika studied nearby at Coventry University and they were close enough to maintain regular contact.

Alexander was a studious person and never had to be told to do his homework. In fact, at times due to his intense desire to do well, he would have to be reminded that the body and brain needed rest. Many books were scattered around the house on how to succeed and influence others and be wealthy in life. This was a mantra, which he carried through to university.

Alexander developed an outward confidence, which could be misconstrued as arrogance, but this was to cover up his shortcomings and his own insecurities.

At college, his poetry writing was almost lost due to the fun and challenges of a young teenager living a fulfilled life. The demands of 'A' Level study and socialising filled the void that had dogged him in the earlier years. He was happy around this period and had shaken off the introspective soul-searching characteristics of the early teenage years where writing was his main release.

However, it was during this period that Alexander began to reveal some of his most intimate writings and despite being encouraged by many to have some published, he always refused, stating that he needed to develop more and they were not to his high standard.

Alexander's interest in politics grew and at the end of his first year at college he had a paid role on the Youth General Council at South Bank as an equal opportunity mentor. His political aspirations were further encouraged by his college lecturers who organised for a group of young people to meet Nick Timothy, the advisor to then Home Secretary, Theresa May, to discuss their views and experience of police stop and search procedures. This led to a meeting with Mrs May. She seemed genuinely concerned about the stories she heard of the overuse of police power and said she and her team wanted to redress the injustice. She sent Alexander a full copy of the Hansard notes when the bill was debated in Parliament.

University Years

Alexander achieved A*AB in his 'A' Levels along with an A* in his Extended Project Qualification (EPQ) thesis where he considered *The Use of Violence and Nonviolent Activity in Bringing about Political Change*. He secured his place at Warwick University to read *Politics, International Relations and Quantitative Methods*.

During Fresher's Week, Theresa May invited Alexander to speak at the Conservative Party conference about stop and search. He eloquently addressed the party for five minutes and had the privilege of introducing the Home Secretary to the stage.

He was grateful that the party was addressing an issue that he felt infringed upon his basic human rights. Alexander recognised the enormity of the platform he had been given and the exposure reignited his passion for poetry, which he developed into performing as a spoken-word poet. In this creative medium, he was able to explore personal and political issues which were topical at the time such as university fees, knife and gun crime, relationship issues, and mental health concerns.

Alexander achieved much in his limited time at Warwick. Following his political debut, his mentor, Nick Timothy, arranged for him to undertake two weeks' work experience at the Home Office. He worked very hard and made lasting impressions. He gave a presentation at the end of the period where he used the opportunity to recite a poem about 'stop and search' to the team including Theresa May. The poem was well received, as it highlighted an uncomfortable relationship with the police despite Alexander acknowledging that he would immediately call upon them if he found himself a victim of crime. However, he was so incensed by their indiscriminate treatment that he had a lifelong suspicion of them.

Connections made during this time led to more work experience in television and political journalism at Sky News. Alexander was introduced to Afua Hirsch, a political commentator who was at the time writing a book to which Alexander contributed as a researcher.

After his time at the home office, Alexander realised he was not yet ready for a political career and began to consider other options. As a people person, he wanted to use his gifts and his developing skills in public speaking for more altruistic purposes. He considered becoming a human rights lawyer or a motivational speaker in addition to a spoken-word poet. He believed gaining personal and business success initially would ultimately bring him worldly experience to assist in a political pursuit later in life. His friends and family joked that he could become the first black prime minister, which tickled Alexander, as being a politician was never his true ambition.

Alexander grew passionate about his desire to help people struggling with mental health issues. He had friends at university who were depressed and unable to share their fears with others. With his own experience he was able to empathise and offer his support.

Alexander praised the ability of women to come together and talk to offload their stress and to support and encourage each other. He lamented that men were afraid to share inner thoughts due to society's expectations of them to be *strong* and *unemotional*.

Alexander was shaken by the suicide of an acquaintance at university and shared how his writings had helped him through a dark period of his life. He said that after he finished his degree, he wanted to set up a charity that would help young men express themselves. He also finally agreed to make public his poetry which he had kept as a personal diary for many years, only occasionally sharing the odd poem with close and trusted friends.

By the second year of university, Alexander was regularly performing spoken-word poetry and had set about planning a publication for an anthology of his work. Such poems would depict the struggle of young black males on the streets, their daily efforts to stay alive and how they were dealing with emotional strain. He wanted to fuse his poetry with classical and/or jazz music to help introduce young people to other genres outside of hip-hop, rap and grime.

As Alexander became friendly with people from all over the world, he wanted other young people to think outside the box and embrace experiences that were not necessarily from their own cultural norms. Sadly, he was not able to develop these ideas as he fell ill in the middle of his second year.

Alexander also found time for fundraising for charity by entering fun runs. In October 2015, he entered the Glasgow half marathon with his mother, raising money for an AIDS testing charity called Grace and Light. He did well and was determined to take up long distance running after he had finished his degree.

The charity was appreciative of his efforts and paid a warm tribute to him when he died. So, too, did Warwick University who, at what would have been Alexander's graduation ceremony, honoured him with a certificate confirming his high academic achievement at the end of his first year. This was a special day for his mother as she proudly accepted the award on behalf of her son.

Family Life

Alexander loved spending time with his extensive family. He was the oldest child to his mother, Joanna, and the second child to his father, Francilien.

He was extremely close to his younger brother, Lamarr, who being more introverted, always looked up to Alexander. In teenage years, the brothers' lives took different paths. Alexander spent much of his time and energy looking out for Lamarr and would encourage him to return to his studies to achieve academic success, which he believed he was so capable of. He always stated that Lamarr would return to education and would become a great individual.

Alexander had a distant relationship with his father who himself had a strict Haitian upbringing where males did not express or show emotions to each other. Alexander, being a sensitive and emotional person, missed having demonstrative affection from his dad. After the marriage breakup, his need for security and emotional approval, sought from his mother, became more apparent. Alexander was close to and admired his maternal uncle, Derek, who was also his godfather. He received a lot of attention from him and was proud that they shared the same zodiac sign, Libra, having their birthdays one day apart.

In his later teen years, Alexander rekindled a closer relationship with his father and began to seek his counsel and wisdom especially during the university days. It was around this period that Alexander began to research his Haitian roots, resuming French lessons which he felt would be advantageous in the increasingly globalised commercial markets. During the last months of his illness, Alexander was happy to see his parents unite for his common good, both praying for a miracle to restore their beloved son back to good health.

Alexander had a photographic memory for remembering people's birthdays, calling friends and family on their day to wish them well. Everyone was amazed at his capacity to recall the dates, which he thought was the norm, and couldn't understand why other people didn't have such a database of birthdays stored in their memory. "A useful trait for studying History and Politics," he would boast. Alexander made the effort to remember personal details during first meetings and would use the information in subsequent conversations with a person demonstrating that he had paid interest in them and what they had to say. This endeared him towards his family and friends.

Alexander wrote several poems about family members and life with them, especially in relation to his mother.

His (half) sister, Christine, being raised in Cardiff, would come to London most summer holidays allowing her to develop a close sibling relationship with Alexander. He confided in her about emotional matters until his later teenage years when his girlfriend, Shanika Wallace, became his sounding board.

Alexander gained great strength from his relationship with his girlfriend, whom he found to have an uplifting nature, ultimately pulling him out of those depressing moods, which were rarely visible outside the confines of his bedroom and certainly masked by his positive disposition.

Alexander loved his cousins and acted as an older brother to the younger females. He also relished talking with his uncles and was proud that he had a great opportunity of growing up with a great-great grandmother who died at the age of 107, shortly after Alexander commenced his chemotherapy treatment. He loved everything about family life.

The Last Battle for Life

Alexander collapsed on Friday 18th March 2016 on the day he was due to go on an educational trip to Belgium. He had spent the night celebrating the end of term. Early the next morning, a friend found him on the bathroom floor having seizures and immediately called an ambulance. He was taken to Coventry Hospital and placed in an induced coma to stop the convulsions which were caused by excessive fluid on the brain.

It was initially believed to be meningitis and Alexander was treated successfully with antiviral and bacterial antibiotics. Three days later, after he came out of the coma and gained 'full recovery', further tests were taken which revealed a lesion on his right temporal lobe — a glioblastoma.

He was transferred to King's College Hospital in London and the decision was taken to perform a lobectomy and biopsy simultaneously. This took place on 9th June 2016. A 'debulking' operation was performed, as the consultant advised that there would be a high risk of brain damage if all was removed due to the tumour having spread to different parts of the brain. The devastating results came a few weeks later when Alexander was diagnosed with stage four malignant glioblastoma.

There are over 30 different types of brain tumours, glioblastoma being one of the most serious types. In the past it was known as the 'graveyard cancer,' as it afflicted older men, however, this is no longer the case as many young children are now being diagnosed. Radiotherapy and chemotherapy can slow down and delay this fast and aggressive deadly tumour although the medical opinion is that it is incurable.

Unfortunately, as much as Alexander displayed a gallant fighting spirit, initially responding well, radiotherapy and subsequent chemotherapy treatments were unsuccessful and the tumour rapidly grew without a period of stability.

In November 2016, doctors advised that the tumour was terminal and they recommended that Alexander's care be transferred to a hospice for better pain management, as he was often in agony. However, his family made a decision to seek alternative therapy at a clinic in Bad Salhausen near Frankfurt in Germany with specialist, Dr Herzog.

In early January 2017, a family friend set up a crowd-funding page to help with the fees for the clinic and over £50,000 was raised within a seven-day period. The response was astonishing and drew media attention, with some journalists contacting Alexander in Germany for an interview with this person who had clearly touched so many people.

This was a very difficult and emotional time for Alexander but despite his trial and the gradual loss of mobility down his left side, he remained positive and inspiring. Alexander's optimistic outlook never wavered, as he stated that there were people in a worse position than him. He said he was glad it happened to him and not his friends, as he felt he was better able to endure the terrible effects the cancer had upon his body. Joanna began to describe Alexander as a 'people magnet,' as she saw how individuals were drawn to him.

His faith as a Christian grew stronger as he encountered the frailty of life. He eventually found peace in himself and exuded confidence, which he strongly believed would help him to deal with his cancer. He knew the odds but refused to dwell on the negative outcome even right to the end.

Alexander so desperately wanted to live as he felt he had so much to contribute to change the world.

After two unsuccessful trips to Germany, Alexander was greatly disappointed that the treatment consisting mainly of hyperthermia and chemoembolization, (heat treatments and low dose chemotherapy directly into the cancerous tumour), had not worked.

His immune system was so compromised that he caught several infections including sepsis, which led to a rapid decline. Alexander's mobility began to deteriorate to the extent that he initially had to use walking aids and eventually, around the end of April 2017, became bedridden and needed constant care. For a proud young man who had been so active and sporty in his youth, it was difficult to accept. However, anyone spending time with him at this period was deeply touched by his gracious spirit and resolve to get through each day and how he continued to uplift and encourage people.

Alexander wanted to return to his full time studies at Warwick University after his operation but was unable to do so. His love for writing and reading also diminished as the months went by. Music, and in particular gospel songs, became his new therapy. Despite the brain cancer, Alexander's cognitive ability was never impaired and he remained able to have deep philosophical conversations about life and world issues. He also continued his love of finding and using new words. A favourite at the time was *phantasmagoria* which his mother thought he had made up until he was able to show and demonstrate its meaning and use. During the early period of illness, Alexander kept a diary documenting his emotions and his growing faith and love of humanity, until he found it difficult to focus and write.

Alexander had achieved some limited success as a spoken-word poet, however, in April 2016 whilst he waited for his brain operation, he attended a gospel fund raising concert at his church and was blown away by the love and support that people showed him. He felt like a celebrity as so many young people came up to him saying that he had inspired them to be a better person. One 12-year-old boy called Azariah was so moved by Alexander that he asked him to be his mentor and later wrote a poem about him after his death.

Had he lived, it was Alexander's ambition to not only reach out and be a mentor to young black boys but to encourage them to do well academically and resist the pull of life on the streets. He was determined that his poems, most of them written during his teenage years into manhood, should be published to help young men struggling with mental health issues and depression. He often acknowledged that his love of writing poems had helped him through a bleak period of life. He was also very determined to be an advocate for young boys to help them resist being groomed into a life of crime and drug dealing.

The pen and paper were Alexander's panacea for healing and addressing deep wounds that hide in one's emotional psyche where, if left unaddressed, they can cause havoc with one's emotions until they become intolerable, with negative consequences. On reading Alexander's vast collection of poems it became apparent that a young man who was always publicly so positive hid an introspective side of his character by transferring his emotions into his written and spoken-word poetry.

Theresa May invited Alexander for tea at Downing Street after his radiotherapy treatment. After he died, Mrs May, as Prime Minister, paid tribute to him in her keynote speech at the 2017 Conservative Party conference, commenting on his inspirational character and acknowledging the contribution he had made and the steps he had taken towards reducing the amount of unlawful stop and search incidents.

Alexander will be remembered as someone who tried to bring about a change in his community and he would have felt honoured to hear his contribution being publicly acknowledged.

Alexander wanted to publish an anthology of his poems to be used in schools to encourage young people away from street life. He hoped they would find another way of expressing themselves in an artistic form such as poetry, music, sports, or art. It was his intention to go into schools, read his poems and speak to young people about choosing to stay on the right educational path from an early age.

Alexander was so determined to get baptised and publicly declared his faith as a Christian shortly after his return from Germany. It was witnessed by a large crowd of family, friends and congregational members who saw him stand up and dance with joy despite his compromised mobility. After this event, he had a brief respite in St Christopher's hospice and in the later stages of his life was helped with support from Marie Curie nurses. His last week of life was spent in Kings College Hospital due to further infections. He had a massive seizure on the Thursday before his death, which eventually compromised his breathing and ability to swallow. On Saturday 3rd June 2017 Alexander died.

Tributes and Extracts

Tributes

7th May 2014

(An extract from the first annual letter written to himself to set the goals to be achieved by the end of that year)

You have performed one poem on the 3rd April 2014 and it was well received. You were congratulated and applauded for your eloquence, story-telling and observation of society, specifically urban areas or ghettoes. By the end of the year, you must have performed five times to showcase your talent but also touch people's souls, liberate people's minds and comfort people's hearts. Respect your talent; take your passion seriously. Poetry is not only a form of expression or escapism but it is also a way of being recognised and potentially paid for the gifts God has blessed you with. Therefore, you must continue this even if it seems hopeless or boring as there is always someone who will seek solace from your words.

October 2016

(Extract from a tribute written by a cancer sufferer who met Alexander in Germany)

"...without my family it was difficult until I met my friend, Alexander. I would never have met him had I not had the "evil" cancer. It was definitely a blessing to have crossed Alexander's path at Dr Herzog's clinic in Germany.

He brought his beautiful energy and light, not only to me, but to everyone around him. His beautiful aura brightened the room and his positive energy was instantly felt by those that crossed his path. I would like to dedicate this entry to my friend, THE BRAVE Alexander King Paul. Thank you so much for giving me the strength during my dark days and now for watching down on me."

Neelam Bains, Cancer survivor; Canada

January 2017

(Extract from a letter sent to Alexander during sickness)

"...at Warwick, you were that hero in the strife. You believe in acting so that each tomorrow finds you farther than today. You will, one day in the distant future, leave those footprints on the sands of time. And I know that for all of us who were fortunate enough to know you, your footprints will always make us take heart again."

Warwick University friend

June 2017

"As was said in so many more eloquent ways at his funeral, Alex made the world a better place in his brief time here, and he will be remembered."

Former History and Politics tutor

October 2017

(Extract from Prime Minister Theresa May's tribute at the Conservative Party conference)

"Alexander spoke so eloquently about his experience and how he came to mistrust those in positions of power as a result.

So inspired by his example, we took action, shook up the system, and reduced the number of black men being stopped and searched by almost a third, with no adverse impact on crime at all."

The Honourable Prime Minister, Theresa May

Extracts from Alexander's notes

16th April 2016

I have so many ideas for my poetry. I really believe I can be great at it and do something different. But not only that, I feel that Jah can use me and my words. I pray that I can execute the ideas I have in my head, the words I have sitting on my heart and make these ideas and words manifest and change the world. I want to inspire, I need to uplift, I have to shine. There's a lot of darkness in this world. I must radiate the rays of the Son/Sun.

5th April 2016

I want to spread love and if it is the Father's will, I will be able to do it! I pray for my brother Lamarr. I love him ever so dearly! I hope his spirit is strong and resilient. I pray that he is using his experience as a time to grow, a time to heal and a time to know himself.

This must be hard on my mother; that celestial being has been through it all but still she stands and remains to be a pillar of comfort and love. Lord, may your plan for her continue to be one rooted in blessings. May I change her life! If it is in your will may I change her life!

I believe I won't die from this. There's more, so much more, for me to do; more to see and more to achieve. More lives to touch and more lives to help. I pray I live.

If not, I pray I live through my words.

3rd April 2016

I have an amazing support system. I am loved. The love, support, care and blessings I am receiving is a testament to who I am. What I mean to people. What I have done and who I am becoming. Father, I pray I can spread more love — please use me as you see fit!

10th October 2015 (written 30 minutes before turning twenty)

As I teeter on the brink of adolescence and adulthood, the end of my teenage years and the start of a new decade, I am grateful. I am grateful for my life, the blessing to be alive is something that leaves me in awe every single day. I am blessed. I am grateful for my friends and family who enrich my life: creating memories that I will forever cherish; comforting and consoling me in times of distress and/or pain but most importantly the constant support and motivation. I am grateful for my girlfriend Shanika Wallace, she is an absolute jewel and I pray that she continues to shine. Whether we make it or not I hope — I want her to know that she brought the most joy and love to my life at times when I was very lonely, depressed and hopeless and for that I will always be indebted to her. I am grateful for all the small things. I am grateful.

...I want to grow spiritually; I pray that I never put my body through any harm that will prevent me from reaching my full potential. I pray that I grow financially too — I want to create a lot of things, which I feel can benefit others, money could be a means to better my life as well as loved ones. However, money isn't everything.

I want to live! I want to live! I want to live!... May I reach my targets and goals? I will reach my targets and goals. I am great. I am amazing. I have purpose. I have a reason to live and I am willing to die for it. I am hopeful. I am a king. I am phenomenal. I am Alexander Maurice Paul.

20th December 2014

I want to be able to bless those that have blessed me. I hope and pray I can do this in all ways. Financial gain will come, it is too easy to make money so I shall not put that on a pedestal and think that is the only way to bless others. I want my heart to be pure.

Most importantly I want and need to grow closer to my Creator, God. I want to put Him at the centre of my life and have a relationship where I trust what He has planned for me. I need to pray more and I need to be more willing to learn about Him.

6th February 2011

My conscience is conscious of the condescending conditions we continue to conform to constantly conflicting our confidence by confabulating contentious utterings but these utterings are never confronted.

February 2011 (written at the back of his poetry book)

If I die tonight, please remember me for the good and the bad. Reminisce on the good qualities and attributes God blessed me with. Explore and analyse the fantastic times we have shared; each one a priceless, unique memory that left an imprint on the history we have shared and created with one another. Remember me as a dreamer and believer; my dreams are the things that have acquainted and transcended the bleak and cloudy barriers of reality with my innovative, imaginative fantasies; my dreams of love, prosperity, peace and happiness for the entire human race to bestow on each other through times of despair and times of joy. Remember me as a believer, a strong, faithful believer in God; the Creator and giver of blessings, the greatest blessing being life. Also a believer that every person is a human being who requires and needs love, affection and understanding, with those three things they can build a foundation of happiness. Please try and remember I tried my best in everything I did.

Do not shy away from my faults because I am plagued by many; an aggressive anger that contradicts my goal of a loving nature and mind-set; my reoccurrences with apathy that deprived and restricted me and my dreams to their full potential. My harsh, discordant words that inflicted pain onto my fellow beings. Please remember we are all sinners and all have dark secrets that we choose to keep hidden. My faults have blessed me in so many ways imaginable but are a controversial and contradictory topic that highlight my qualities and demean them at the same time. But I did try my best.

If I die tonight I have no regrets, although my life has mixed and been influenced by sin and illicit doings. I have lived, laughed, loved, and learnt. Surrounded by beautiful souls, disappointed that I have annoyed or agitated a few but that is how life is. But I pray tonight; hoping that you'll enjoy life and make the world a better place. If I die tonight, I pray I will spend the beginning of forever with my Saviour.

But that's only if I die tonight; I still want to change my faults and the world!

Extract from his most eminent Poetry "I am Love"

I was climbing clouds
Catching comets,
Callously as my calluses could not burn...
As I clasped, into the corners of the sun...

I was the laughter,
The laughter of the school children
Carefree and naïve
Before they realised they could
Never afford to pay the university tuition fees...

You see I am the thing that will survive your very existence,
Commemorating your life with passion and persistence,
I am the thing that makes you feel,
I AM LOVE

Alexander Paul

PART 2

ANTHOLOGY OF POEMS

Plant a Seed of Peace

Plant a seed of peace
Water it with love and happiness
Don't let the evil in the world destroy it
Keep away trespassers
Scare away birds of prey
Harvest peace
Now a beautiful blue flower of peace
Joy and love blooms
Peace is like a puzzle.

15th July 2005

Her Everlasting Knowledge and Beauty

Like other girls
She has beauty and knowledge.
She knows her beauty may fade away
But her knowledge will last another day.
Although this is true in most cases
And it may happen to most faces
But not her face, her face is
Like her knowledge
It is endless.
Hopefully I can be the one who can tell her
That her beauty and knowledge shall remain together
And she shall stay in my heart 'til the end of forever.

3rd January 2010

Emancipation

My people have been emancipated for over 100 years
Yet I do not feel like a free man
I've seen black mothers cry a thousand tears
We tried the best we can
For our freedom
But our oppressors subjugate us
We are abused, disrespected and shunned
My people are treated like dust
We always ask this question
When will the black man
Truly get his emancipation?

We have been brainwashed to believe we are free
And that everyone is treated equally
Racism is still alive and I wish I could choke it
Because it's plague on humanity has made us sick
Why should I get persecuted for the complexion of my skin?
As soon as they see me, they think I'm about to sin
We have been brought up to believe we are free
But do you see people surrounded by equality?
Or do you long for the day when we can live as one
And no race has to be shunned
So I am still asking this question
When will the black man truly get his emancipation?

5th September 2010

Drugs Stole My Sanity

This life I'm living is getting crazier and crazier
I don't know if it's the weed or the schizophrenia
I drown in the concept because it's too deep
I'm losing my mind, my thoughts and my own sleep
I see images of the dead, paranoia's stuck my head
I'm too scared, I just can't sleep in my own bed
My mind is darker than melanin
Pain is locked deep within
The life I'm living is full of sin
There's needle marks on my skin
I talk to God; he's not answering
Now I'm lost and there is no one to find me
The spirit's low, there is no-one to guide me

I wake up in my vomit; I ain't been feeling too well
They say I'm on Earth but I know I'm in hell
No one trusts me but I don't even blame 'em
How'd you trust a junkie who is covered in phlegm?
So I beg on the streets; every sentence ends with *please*
The strength in my feet are gone, I'm relying on my knees
But people walk and stare in disgust
Although disgust should be replaced by distrust

I know why they don't trust me
Cos all I'll do is spend it on coke and LSD
Every day is a struggle, I long to be free
Where weed and coke no longer travel with me
Where pain and sorrow are no longer friendly

I know I am not dignified
The drugs I use stole my pride
I need help I'm falling' into a dark abyss
Filled with anguish and hate, never beauty and bliss
The way I'm living I won't survive
Will I ever see twenty-five?
My days on this earth are getting shorter and shorter
My life's a bad book, I am the author
It's times like these I think of euthanasia
This life I'm living is getting crazier and crazier
I know it's the weed and I know it's the schizophrenia

5th October 2010

Unappreciated Skin, Unappreciated Features

His skin was the colour of the darkest coal.
He saw being black as something to be abused,
Pain and anger were engraved on his soul.
He looks down at his hands and he was never enthused.

His curly kinky hair was always hard to comb
And this was all because he was black.
He felt caged and there was no place to roam
He felt his skin was meant to be under attack.

He called his thick lips those slugs under his nose.
His nose was that fat tube stuck on his face
These things always got in the way; they seemed to impose.
They were a sign of ugliness; a sign of disgrace

He thought his skin kept him behind.
He felt it made him subjugated,
The type of skin you would not confide in
He always felt he was unappreciated.

But he did not realise his black beauty.
He chose to abuse and hate himself
The black nation has overcome cruelty.
But he is oblivious to his natural wealth.

He believes his skin stops his dreams from being in reach,
So he hides and tries to shelter himself from all
He has now damaged his beauty due to bleach,
Because he did not know, being black is beautiful.

They say the darker the berry, the sweeter the juice,
And the darker the skin, the deeper the roots.
So don't let no-one tell you black isn't beautiful,
Your skin belongs to you, so make sure you are comfortable!

8th October 2010

Unique Vulnerability

I am that individual who is afraid of being homogenous,
Never that individual seeking to be an individual like everyone else
It may sound confusing, a bit bamboozling
But it's misunderstood just like myself.
There have been accusations about my mental health,
Whether my philosophy should be stuck on the shelf.
Misconceptions of me are forever flying around my head,
If I wasn't emotionally strong I'd be swimming in tears I just shed
It seems I am forever isolated,
I confide in solitude because of the beauty of reality.
My dreams and thoughts are my jealous friends,
Who hold animosity to society.
So I am alone on this wondrous creation from God,
Trying to find someone to connect to
But it's hard when human nature and confusion seep through,
Which I've never been used to
My heart aches for the acceptance of these so-called men,
I long for this day so please tell me when.
I wish I could cry and feel the emotions of these people,
But I can't do this because I'm never fearful.
I long for that day when someone can understand me,
To let me out of this cage of paranoia and set me free
I long for that day when I'm never alone;
Sitting in a corner in my cold, empty home.
I long for that day when my dreams and thoughts
Can mingle with humanity
To help take away my powerful insanity
But today is not that day; when will that day come?

Will it come when I'm strong and when my heart is feeling numb?
I never thought of it like that,
My life used to be bright now it's turning black
My uniqueness has become my weakness,
So I am led to think that I am a figment of your imagination.
I am ambiguous, I am never clear
I'm merely a part of your atmosphere.
I'm that aura that is always lingering
I am nobody. I am that thing.

19th October 2010

Cries From the Youth

There is pain out here but I got to continue
The floor stained with blood but it's not an issue
There ain't no time for me to show fears
My friend died yesterday but I didn't shed no tears
The streets need me, I'm that yute that they follow
The whole concept is too hard to swallow
The government don't do nothing to help the situation
All these yutes have a great frustration.
Were trapped in that disgusting system
We are not living, we're just existing

The pain I see is stuck on my face
To my parents I am that disgrace.
The corrupted police arrest any youth
Even if the yute is speaking the truth
The streets have made our hearts cold
Certain yutes don't even see 16 years old
Will things ever get better?
Or will the concrete continue to get redder?

I can't wait for the day when the yute will smile.
It's been too long; it's been a while.
I want to see the knife crime go down
Hopefully I'll still be around.
Most of us are good, some educated
So why are we seen as bad, why are we hated?
We are still young so come and guide us
We need help and we need your trust

Stop arresting us for stupid reasons
We get persecuted in all four seasons.
Our souls are tired, we need rest
We are accused of things we haven't done, it doesn't make sense
I'm tired of running from the police
Always trying to show my innocence.
I am a black male speaking the truth
I'm also a percentage of the youth.

Everything I've said is true
I don't care if you're an adult,
I have the same rights as you!

28th October 2010

"Daddy Do You Still Love Me?"

"Daddy do you still love me?" that's what I used to say to him
He replied with silence, he looked at me with those dark brown eyes
And my heart trembled with violence because he didn't hear my cries
My skin got goose bumps being around him,
I used to wish he took me to the park
Kick some ball, we could have had a laugh, but everything was so dark
My mind was never at rest contemplating whether his love was ever real
He always kept that hidden deep in his chest, never to be revealed
So I constantly wondered whether my daddy loved me
In my dreams he showered me with love, but never in reality
So my years of growing up were very confusing
I never understood this figure
He was a righteous man who walked upright, never seen as that "Nigger"
But throughout my childhood fatherly love never surrounded me
Was it my fault or his? This question stains my mind entirely
My years of asking whether his love follows me have stopped
Now his years of asking whether I love him, have started
See how the roles have swapped,
But my years of hatred have now departed
Because his love was shown in a different way, I could not grasp
My words were once wasted for all the years I asked
He shined his love in a way that I could not hear
He taught me valuable lessons and to never fear
He taught me lessons where my heart could feel
Even teaching me lessons for my pride to heal
For my pride and confidence was hurt
Not knowing the answer to my question
Even though he was the central figure for my question's direction

Although I never did vent out my frustration with no demonstrations
His heart finally connected to my pain and sent signals to his brain
He acknowledged the years that his words never shone
But now I realise words are less than actions
And that mysterious figure who I descend from
Is the man I shall continue to love until I'm dead and gone
You may say he showed his love wrong
But in fact he is the one who has made me strong
Now the roles have switched, I'll answer your question gladly
The thing I got to say is I "love you, my daddy "

4th November 2010

Me and You Are the Same

I'm homeless, hopeless, I live outside Tesco
When your kids walk by you say "come on children let's go"
I wonder why you do this? Why do you scold me?
So I wait outside for another passer-by to walk past me
But you don't, you cross the road so you don't choke on my stench
The only shelter I have is under that nearby bench
I beg and plead for your money, not for greed but to feed my hunger
Your eyes stare into mine and see that I'm not fine and howl with laughter
You still do not have a penny to spare even though you wear that Gucci suit
Your little girls' eyes acknowledge the pain I'm going through
I have no clean close to protect my skin from the punishing sun
You clearly see my feet have no shoes on them, you had to be oblivious
I'm here every day, here's where I lay. This is where I stay
I have no house but this is my home, right in front of Tesco is where I roam
But you still see the conditions I am living in,
To the point where cockroaches crawl on my skin
You look at me and quickly look away,
Your hands continue to hold your wallet
But I say you're very lucky, because there's no money in my pocket
How longer will you continue to avoid me? I have no food to sustain me
So I stay on my knees, but your hand does not help as if I have a disease
I have not eaten in days, days turn to weeks, I still can't stand on my feet
Whilst you walk past me every day with the suitcase in one hand,
An apple in the other
But you continue to see me starving, my stomach forced to suffer
How much longer will you resist me, how long will you pass?
This is a question I have to ask

You say you don't help me because I don't help myself
You believed that I sniffed cocaine and destroyed my physical health
You see my runny nose, mucus touching my lips, and think
I've always been unclean
So you think that I abused my nose and lived the life of the fiend
Your daughters look at me and see the fear in my eyes
Whilst you act surprised, thinking I should be ashamed of these lies
You foolishly think I am degrading myself to steal your money
I laugh at your ignorance because I think this is funny
No money in the world could buy my dignity forcing me to live outside a shop
Where everybody's eyes drop and they stop and stare at me
But no money comes towards me
The life I lead is terrible yet you think I do it to 'con' the nation
People like you, sir, intensify my frustration
Because I was like you, I had a good job and a good life
I was always greeted at home by some cooked food and a good wife
Until the day I got fired at work couldn't pay the bills
The stress got my wife, she got addicted to those pills
The doctors took her away from me and I had nowhere to stay
That is why you see me outside this shop... today
And I believe the main reason I'm here is the same reason you avoid me
Because I was once disgusted by some beggar in poverty
So before you judge me today and walk away
I would like to teach you a lesson because life is a bitch
You could be that beggar like me, we might just switch!

5th November 2010

All Because His Father Left

He is now shottin white to make his future bright
His mother doesn't know but she wouldn't think it's right,
He started trapping on da streets every day and night
Until the pigs come he's ghost so he's out of sight.

He had dreams of gettin outta dis ghetto,
But the controlling system just won't let go
He knows this ain't the good life but it's the only life he knows.
He's kinda dirty just like his own stinkin clothes
His mum lost her job she's trying the best she could
But your best ain't nuttin whilst you're living in da hood.
Her son ain't goin to school, where's his education?
Shottin white and hustlin is his only dedication.
She's lost all hope; she is struggling to pay the bills.
The worst thing is she's addicted to those pills
She's trying hard to stay clean, to provide for her 16-year-old
She asks why life has been so damn cold.

Life wasn't always like this.
Nah fam, it was filled with happiness and bliss
Until his father walked out the door.
Just to make babies with some dirty whore.
There used to be times when we used to smile
But that was back when he was just a little child
Now that smile turned to a dirty screw.
Same shit, different day, there ain't nothing new.
Not a lot of friends he trusts, there's only a few
And all this is because his father walked out the door

His emotional scars won't heal so they're still sore
The life without that father figure got bad, so he got mad
Forcing his mother to become sad, so he sells white to buy stuff he never had
The streets have become his new dad
So he's become loyal to his new dad, spending hours with him
Even if his new dad causes him to sin
So he does stuff his mama wouldn't be proud of
But he's gotta do this so he doesn't have to starve

He wonders how life would've been if his father hadn't gone
Ever since he left everything's been wrong
His mum is choking on them pills, can't pay the bills and has no job skills
Whilst he's selling cocaine, trapped in the game
Wondering if things will be the same

So his mum is addicted to those pills; and he's addicted to these streets
He wonders will you ever smile again, and if so,
WHEN?

6th November 2010

So What is My Name?

I have a name which is not mine but I use it on legal notes
My culture, religion and beliefs were stripped away from me.
My male ancestors were emasculated of their names,
White slave masters raped theirs and my women.
But refused to be a dad to their black offspring.
So my name is not mine, so I am living a lie
My mother says those not living the truth must die
So should I die, forcing my family members to cry, all because I'm living a lie?
No!
Because I am a negro which is close to necro which means death
But I shall overcome death till I breathe my very last breath.
I shall overcome slavery, I shall overcome poverty and I shall overcome apathy.
I am not hateful towards the slave masters or the white man for my sister
Is half white and that would not be right, contradicting my family
Out of blind fury and aggressive spite.
I am only angry because my name is not mine so I can't leave an imprint
On history, humanity, reality or society.
If my 'name' is mentioned it'll be the false me, the name not of my ancestry
So I have great pain, not because my name won't gain any fame
But because my name won't show how I overcame shame
By wearing those chains.

I have lost everything even my own name
I have lost everything even my own name
I have lost everything even my own name.
So what is my name?

I don't know. I don't even know my own name

8th November 2010

My Darling Chicken

Your sweet succulent size caress my taste buds
You're my addiction but I could never have too much
I love it when my tongue kisses your skin
Whilst I gaze at your brown legs on the table in my kitchen
I have enjoyed your company for all my life
That's why I never hurt your feelings, never using a knife
Your breasts bring happiness to my mouth whilst I suck on them
I want you all to myself never sharing with friends
I'm always in the mood to dine with you
Especially if you have 'make-up' on, sorry this is true
I love massaging your skin especially with seasoning
My mind blows when your perfume lingers around my home
I feel better when it's just you and me alone
I get angry because brothers can't treat you right, they always waste
But I know you love it when I have you, I see it in your face
Baby can't you see I need you, I love you too much
I love your thighs, your breasts and I even love your touch
I can't live without you, you're the only one I trust
It's not just love, I have passion and lust...
For you.
I've even introduced you to my mum
Baby! Can't you see you're my number one?

8th November 2010

64

This is My Blood on the Page

These lyrics are part of me, this is my blood on the page
These lyrics will vary from happiness to emotional rage
The pen I write with is filled with my blood and tears
Helping me paint pictures of emotions I felt over the years
My blood stains the page as my lyrics are from my heart
These lyrics will last forever because emotions never depart
My memories are spilt out on this page, helping you understand me
My dreams dance on these sheets of paper helping you know I'm happy
So don't be afraid by the blood on this page
And smile with my happiness and cry from my rage
I pray you get an emotional connection from the words I have said
Because these lyrics are memories taken from my head

These lyrics last forever they have no age
Do not be afraid of the blood staining this page

9th November 2010

Conversations With the Wall

I keep on having conversations with the wall
But it never replies
So my words bounce back and hit my eyes
And I realise I have no one else to talk to
I'm lonely
I keep on talking to the wall hoping it'll reply
I've been doing it for ages, years have gone by
And it still does not say hello
So I have no want to talk about my pain and sorrow
In fact, pain that encases my soul has made me hollow
But I am a persistent person continue to talk to the wall.
Even when I'm hurting, the wall still says nothing at all
So I'm surrounded by silence although I shout at it
"Talk to me, talk to me! Please, why don't you talk to me
But it does not hear my cries, it refuses to speak
Knowing this makes my confidence weak, vulnerability begins to leak
So this wall has the cheek
The audacity to ignore me
Easily blowing away my authority
I can't understand it, it still bemuses me
How an inanimate object refuses to talk to me!
The confusion of this still confuses me
How something not real makes me seem fake
The wall I tried to talk to I now hate
So now man should appreciate
The fact he is not the greatest thing living
Try talking to a wall; you'll never end up winning

12th November 2010

My Fight Against Pain

I wear a disguise, an exterior, façade
Not to appear different
But because I know it's hard
To penetrate my skin with pain
Or to let it hurt my heart
Forcing me not to love again and letting rage depart
Because I don't want pain to violate my skin
Or for it to hurt my heart locked deep within
Because I've seen too much pain around me
It hurts my eyes and there's no surprise
Why I don't want to be involved with pain
Because I could not go on or sustain
Knowing my heart's been burnt by fiery lies
Or the fact it's pierced my skin with painful knives

Why would I put myself through that?
That's why I'm in a bubble
That keeps me safe from pain and all of that trouble
That's why I struggle to understand the concept of pain
Because I do not want to paint to drain my happiness
Which would then make my heart restless, relying on antidepressants
So pain can drift away from me because I don't need it
But pain won't do that, it'll last forever
Fortunately, me and pain will never be together
Because my disguise has made me invincible
Unusually invisible so pain cannot torment me
I can live with happiness and joy
I can finally be free

12th November 2010

Aggressive Words

This anger made me hate the wrong person
My anger is making me break everything, soon to break the news
This fiery anger is burning my victims but I refuse to say sorry
Only because my anger has taken over my sensible thoughts
So I move viciously without thinking
My anger hurts even me, so I'm aching
From the bitter words I spray at you
My flaming hate will burn like the sun
Whilst my aggressive words will pierce me like a bullet from a gun
But I hate my anger because it's made me hate you
So when I'm angry I see you in a different view
And this is the thing that I regret most
Because when I said "I hated you" that's when you acted like a ghost

13th November 2010

The Caged Bird

I know why the caged bird sings
Even though it's trapped within these metal bars
It smiles even though its wings have scars
And his eyes doodle when it sees the stars
Although it's trapped and hope seems far away
Its positive mind thinks of a brighter day
Its heart longs to go outside and play
But locked within this cage is where it shall stay

I know why the caged bird sings
Although it's trapped and its heart hugs sorrow
The caged bird dreams of the new tomorrow
Where it can spread its wings and fly
It's been caged for too long but it has to try
So it can roam through the majestic sky
And hover freely as people go bye

I know why the caged bird sings
It sings for the right to freedom
Its emotions have been suppressed for too long
The caged bird is forced to think it's done wrong
Although the bird's body is weak, its heart is strong
The caged dreams of better days a brighter tomorrow
So it can say its goodbye to all its sorrow
The caged bird is a beautiful soul
But society has subjugated it and taken control
The caged bird longs to be free
If you're wondering how I know
The caged bird is me

15th November 2010

Ghetto Dreams

They said dreams were not allowed in the ghetto
I break that law every day so please call me a criminal
I dream dreams no one seems to realise
My dreams are shy; only seen by my eyes
My dreams also revolutionise
The typical dreams, so you'll be surprised
I dream dreams with everything is right
No skin colour, no black and white
Where the sun's yellow teeth shine so bright
And the moon's perfect glow eliminates the night
The white cotton candy is situated in the sky
The truth is accepted, there is no need to lie
Where people have no limitations, we can even fly
We can even laugh with God so we don't have to die
These dreams are a way or get away from evil
Where lies on more than lies, their more deceitful
My dreams are a wonderful paradise
A place where laughter's the language, doesn't that sound nice?
I wish you could enter my dreams and realise
But dreams are illegal in the ghetto, so you'll be institutionalised
But break the law and become a criminal
They tried to stop me but they can't stop us all
Dream dreams that are beyond humanity
Dream dreams that are beyond our own sanity
Dream dreams that come alive in your sleep
Dream dreams that become morally deep
Dream dreams and they'll come true some way
Keep dreaming dreams, we'll get out of this prison some day!

16th November 2010

Happiness of a New-born Baby

Happiness of a new-born
The acts of happiness
The act of joy
Whether it's a girl or boy

The wide smile that can't be erased
The love for a new-born baby that can't be replaced
The tears rolling down your eyes
Laughter as soon as the baby cries
Happiness for the rest of your life.

20th November 2010

I Like My Smile

I let my smile tickle my mouth until I end up laughing
I try let my happiness be shown
I try to let my happiness be known
I let my laughter be the language my heart it speaks
And my smile the key to open up her happiness
My I be happy throughout my life
May my smile be my protection from pain and strife

20th November 2010

The Alien

I'm feeling kind of sad today so I don't feel to rhyme
I don't even have the words to express how I feel
There is not enough time
But I guess I've become so used to rhyming that it oozes out in all my writing
I just feel like no one understands me
I try to do right but I make people angry
I'm a good hearted person who loves to smile and make jokes
But I'm cursed with a curse and my emotions go out of control
So I smile to hide the pain that I'm feeling
It's good to let your emotions out but I never reveal them
The only time you'll realise my pain is when my emotions spill out on the page
But I gossip and talk too much but my secrets remain hidden
I wish I could cry but I can't; it's been six years since I cried
I try to but I can't waste my tears
Because that would be ungrateful for the life I have
So my tears are unemployed waiting for their new job
But no event has been diligent enough to book an appointment
I tried expressing how I feel,
It was personal but that idiot went on and told them all
So that the trust has vanished; I live alone
You may think I'm over exaggerating but I'm not
I just feel lonely
Alone with me, myself and I
But you don't know it, only the paper and pen do
I haven't gained enough trust to invest in you
So I am an enigma, the youth who is mysterious
My emotions and secrets are locked up but where is the key?
The person who walks the streets looking for someone at night

But isn't successful
I shall be like this till you understand me
But now I think I am an alien
Too weird for the world
A secretive alien who seems to be alone
My worst fear is dying alone so I have to find someone quickly
Before it's too late
I don't want to die before my time
I don't want to die as that alien
I have become a vulnerable thing
I am the sad alien who is trapped in the wrong planet

22nd November 2010

The Valley of Death

I casually stroll through the valley of death
Never knowing when I'll breathe my last breath
If I die now my soul will be at rest
And I'll be put to the test
Will I go to heaven or hell?
Only time will tell
Shall I smile with God
Or should I cry with Satan?
That is the question everyone is debating!

23rd November 2010

I Broke her Heart

I broke your heart
They kept on talking
She kept stalking
But it wasn't easy
I broke your heart
Our love was to depart
I'm the guy that made her start
Taking those drugs
Now she has sex with thugs
No love, no hugs
She doesn't care she just shrugs
And continues to hurt
I made her feel like dirt
She's nothing, what is she worth?
This all happened because I broke your heart
Now my mind is stuck in the dark
Memories are trapped in the past
Our love was never to last
So our love was doomed from the start
It ended with me breaking her heart

24th November 2010

A Turbulent Friendship with Satan

I only go to church to make my mum smile
Cos I know it's been a while
And she knows I've been jamming with Satan
I need saving cos I'm always misbehaving
But I ain't changing
Because I refuse to see the error of my ways
I am having doubts whether I should give God praise
My heart's not in the mood for change
It's in the mood for rage
Mamma says I'm acting strange
She says it's just a phase
So she arranges a day at church
For my soul to search and find God
But has he ever been lost?
So I went, nothing was changing
Cos ever since I've been jamming with Satan
I've been hating and lost the relationship with God
Now I'm in the devil's playground
And I'm his best friend
We never talked but cos
I walked away from God
Me and Satan got tight
He put me on the wrong road so now I'm leaving, right

It's a bad life I'm leading
My heart is bleeding with sin
This is always feeding Satan
I don't want to jam with him

Because it's making my mamma cry
I keep on asking why can't Satan die?
He taught me how to lie
So I know why the truth still hides
Satan's destroying my life but I still
Decide to ignore Christ
And that ain't nice
So Satan's my malignant best friend
He's behind my back
As I write with this pen
God still wants me back
But I lack of self-control
Satan tickles my soul
I tried to be good, but Satan won't let go

So Satan's my best friend; but he's not good
God is asking me to come back; I think I should
Mama's crying again; wipe her tears away? I wish I could
My mind and my life is so misunderstood

I need saving
With Satan I misbehaving
I think it's time for changing
But my heart is still hating
Will I go to heaven or hell?
People are debating
This is too much to take in

27th November 2010

This Ain't a Game

Ayo 'lil' man, I heard you're trying to get into the game
Don't you know the game brings pain?
I can't explain the pain that's involved in this game
And yet you want to enter, are you insane?
On these streets, I've been here for years and
I shed tears because I've had so many fears
My mind is not mine, the streets took it away
My faith is lost; I have no time to pray
Where has the time gone? The streets made me old
The thug life has made my heart cold
My life is dirty and I'm gathering mould
My life is in danger so my gun is the only thing I hold
And you still want to enter this game,
Ain't you been told,
That there are friends out here looking for that next drug?
I'm still alive on the streets and it's down to the luck
Because it's risky out here
Blood sweat and tears round here
Every day I confront my fears and
My mum shed tears cos she knows I'm doing wrong
She goes to church and sings a song and wishes
I could be her son, the one that protects her
From terror, not the one that creates danger
I've lost everyone; I'm the only one left
Most of my friends in pen; got a couple years left
But some are 6 feet in the ground
How does that sound?
If I continue like this, I won't be around

I'm not proud because I got blood on my hands
And it's not mine, so I have a dirty conscience
And it doesn't make sense, how my presence
Can cause pain and make blood
Stains on the floor
This life I lead is not a game; do you still want to play?
If your mum knew what would she say?
Cos I broke my mum's heart more than enough
And the reason is cos I'm on these streets
And the streets are tough
I've had enough but I'm stuck
In the system where I am a thug
So I'm addicted to the streets
You could say it's my drug
Hey blud, get your education
Stay in school
Be an inspiration to these yutes
Speak the truth
Learn, love and laugh
Make your mum proud
Cos mine's had enough
Of the pain I've caused
Don't be stuck in this system
Where the thugs don't live
We just exist in
This concrete jungle
Where danger lurks and our hearts hurt
Don't be like us, use your brain
Don't get trapped in the game
And inflict pain on yourself

And your mum
Cos life ain't fun
You don't want to be another one
Lost to this life
Because your skin got pierced by a knife
Keep smiling and don't cause any pain
Ask yourself this question
Do you still want to enter this game?

29th November 2010

Unrecognised Wealth of a Queen

I close my eyes and I see your beauty
And then I open my eyes and realise you are priceless
You're not worthless, even though you're worth less than silver and gold
They got it wrong because they priced you to less
You could be penniless and still be rich
Rich in character, rich in elegance and rich with grace
The beauty you radiate enriches my soul
So I can put a smile on your face
I am so grateful to have you
That's why I continue
To go to school to make your dreams come true
I want to make enough money
So you don't have to work no more
I'll make enough money so you never get in debt
Because my life is in debt to you
For giving birth to my big head
Although I do not have any money
I'm the richest boy alive
Because I have you as a mother
And this is why I strive
To make you smile
To make you proud
You're the reason I'm allowed
To be the richest boy in the world
I want to shower you with diamonds and pearls
But I can't, so I wait
Wait for the time to
Show you how much I appreciate

The years you cared for me and my brother
You are an incredible mother
You are the greatest asset I do not own
A Royal Queen on her rightful throne (at home)
You truly deserve a crown
I love you Ms Joanna Diana Brown (a.k.a. mum)

2nd December 2010

I Can't Cry

I don't cry. Why waste your tears?
Because what happens when another bad event comes in a few years?
I've shed tears but it doesn't ease my pain
And those waterfalls coming from my eyes stain
My face for all to see it
But what if my pain was a secret
And I chose not to reveal it?
That means my teardrops are intruders of emotions;
My feelings
Always stealing my despair
And trying to make you care
So you spread sympathy and affiliate with empathy
But this is useless
Because you never understand me
My pain is not the same as yours
My tears are a disease that needs to be cured
So I'm dying with pain
And my eyes are aching with this acid liquid
My eyes have now become a victim
So I choose not to participate in an act
That shows the abuse I've been going through
My eyes can't forgive those tears
So what am I supposed to do?

I can't cry, the rain does it for me
I don't waste my tears
Because they would not be valuable
My tears are precious gems that I create

But they were made from pain, so I hate them
If you want, come and take them
Because then you'll see the pain that I see
And maybe you could understand me
Without affiliating with empathy
You'll feel the pain that I feel
That I try to conceal and never reveal
Each teardrop carries a story
Do you want to read it?
My tears are hungry for the chance to come out of the cage
And to illustrate my pain; my rage
Do you want to feel it?
I have tried to cry
Especially when my friends have died
But the tears always seem to hide
Although I don't cry, I want to
I want you to know that I tried
And my heart aches inside
But I just can't cry
Please help me cry

4th December 2010

I Can Hear Those Demons, Can You?

I hear voices that are not even there
Only I hear them because they whisper in my ears
Trying to take over me and interrogate my fears
But don't you hear? Don't you hear them?
And don't you fear? Don't you fear them?
I'm scared of these voices travelling around my head
These voices are murderers and they want me dead
Are you sure you don't hear these voices?
I do and they're creating these strange noises
My eyes are seeing images of death
These voices are breathing down my neck, don't you feel the breath?
They're after me and they want my soul
I'm an animal stuck in a deep hole
A mouse caged in a locked trap
Can't you hear them? They are back to get me
These voices after me, can you save me?
I hear these voices and I follow
Don't... don't you hear them too?
Are these same voices after you?
They're even outside waiting for me
I can't go outside; I'm in captivity
These demons won't let me
These voices won't let me free
My eyes can only see the death of me
I can't trust no one, they're all after
I'm stuck in my house but there is no safety
Don't you feel their presence?
I can; they are touching my skin

Whispering in my ear is to
Corrupt what's deep within
Can you help me?
Do you see them?
Do you believe me?
Do you fear them?
I can hear those Demons

4th December 2010

If U Don't Listen, You Must Feel

They say I'm clever and they say I'm wise
To this I'm confused, I am quite surprised
Because when I was young, I think I was five
I was the boy who stuck his willy to his flies
Yeah I know it was a stupid mistake
One you should never make
But I was curious
I want to know if it was true
How super was ordinary superglue?
So I climbed up the chair in the kitchen
My mum told me not to do this
But I never listened
And I found the cabinet where mum hid the glue
As soon as I saw it, I knew what to do
I couldn't use my hands because that would peel off my skin
So I thought, let me use the thing that is dangling
It was brilliant a stroke of genius
So I added a streak of glue and added it to my penis
I connected it to my thigh
Oh why, why did I add it to my thigh?
Because I found the wrath of super glue
It's rightfully called super and it's true
It was a struggle because I didn't want to rip skin
In the back of my mind, I always knew this was a bad thing
I didn't want my mum to know so I didn't cry
Because if she knew I was surely about to die
She would've slapped me and hit my backside
Hit me so hard I would've lost all my pride

I eventually took my willy out of that situation
And this was thanks to serious concentration
There were no scars so it didn't need to heal
Mamma always said 'if you don't listen, you must feel!'

4th December 2010

Memories Never Die

Why'd you do that shit, what were you thinking?
You've made your mum cry, now her heart is sinking
I can't believe you're gone; my eyes are still blinking
Because I see images of you
Now I'm always thinking
Of the good times we used to share
Back in the times when we played truth or dare
But those are memories I can't get back
You always told me 'get money and stack
High, and make it reach the sky
So you and ma can live a good life'
But you're not around to tell me that
I told you that 'I love you and I got your back'
I wish you were back but there's no back to rely on
Ever since you left, my shoulders have been the one your ma cries on
You haven't left the country, you left the Earth
Now we realise how much you were worth
You were a good yute
Who always spoke the truth
But now six feet on the ground: your missed
I'll never see you again and I'm pissed
Cos we were too close to be friends, we were brothers
Even if we didn't have the same mothers
You didn't even get to see mine
But don't worry, you don't have to say sorry
I want to tell people how you died
But you died shamefully
And I don't want people judging you

Cos I'll react angrily
Just know that I got you even though you're dead
I keep seeing you dying and it's messing up my head
Just know that I got you even though you're dead
Rest your head on the pillows in the sky
Just know that memories never die

5th December 2010

The Forgotten Friend

Do you feel the pain tormenting his heart?
Do you see the tears in his eyes?
Did you see love leave and depart?
Did you cover the truth with your lies?
Does it hurt? Did you realise its worth?
You say you'll give a helping hand
But do you really understand?

6th December 2010

My Muslim Friend

She said Asalaam alaikum
That means *peace unto you*
But it's not working
My heart is still aching, still learning
But the pain that encases my soul is breaking
But I am still yearning to smile
But she says it one more time
Asalaam alaikum
And I felt the blessings shower upon me
And now I'm smiling for that rest of eternity
Because the peace is surrounding me
I feel innocent just like a little child
When she said 'Asalaam alaikum'
She made my heart smile.

6th December 2010

She Shall Rise Up One Day

She shall rise up one day
Abandoned slavery but restricted by mental chains
Mother to the people of the world
Although they do not appreciate her worth
Even though they put her through an agonising birth
A bittersweet history that has been overcome

She shall rise up one day
Stricken by grief and poverty
Malnourished by the bad economy
Watching the children starve in silence
Because she is too old to bear youthful fruit
She has been crippled by her desolation

She shall rise up one day
Although she is aching from political injustice
She cries from the effects of corruption
Her heart longs for a righteous son to lead
A man that the people will follow
And take away her heart's sorrow
She shall rise up one day
She will be free from mental slavery
She will overcome corruption
She will emancipate herself from political injustice

She shall rise up one day
Rise from your knees Mama Africa!!!

7th December 2010

The Only One Alive

Have you ever felt that you're the only one alive?
And every day is a struggle for you to survive
Whilst the secrets you keep in your mind
Are eating at you as they decay inside
You ain't got time to lie or tell the truth
So emotions leave; no longer by your side
This all happens when you're the only one alive

7th December 2010

The Beach

My toes are sleeping in the sandy blanket
Whilst my eyes are gazing at the women in bikinis.
What a beautiful scenery!
The sun's yellow teeth are shining
Just as soon as the women get in the ocean
What perfect timing.

The women swim delicately just like mermaids
My mum sees me staring at them
So she tells me to behave
But I can't,
They are just too beautiful.

The women in the sea have captured my eyes
It looks like a fantasy
But it is actually reality
But these women are too old for me
They are beyond my reach
But I don't mind.
I still love the beach.

9th December 2010

Do I Have Enough Money to Enrol for Uni?

I can't believe you are restricting me from my education.
Emasculating me from a great future
A future filled with achievements and prosperity.
But how can this be
If I don't have enough money to enrol for Uni?

University would be the foundation
To the start of my aspirations
After years of education
But how can this be
If I don't have enough money to enrol for Uni?

A great way to socialise and meet new friends,
But I'm currently living with suspense.
I keep on asking myself,
Do I have enough money to go to Uni?

To have the chance to meet people who are friendly
But since you have raised the fees,
This does not seem likely
Do I have enough money to enrol for Uni?

Do you want to make me a recluse?
Or a person who will be reckless?
You cannot expect there to be no violence
The youth will not suffer in silence.
So I will become reckless,
Aggravating you till you become restless
All because I don't have enough money to enrol for Uni?

I am speaking as a member of the youth
Consequently, I am speaking the truth
This is disgusting
What you are doing to the future generation
Most of the youth will be in deprivation, for their education
You are stealing their hopes, dreams and aspirations
Which were constructed from sheer dedication.

Do I have enough money for my education?
Do I have enough money for University?
Do I have enough money to enrol for Uni?
Answer these simple questions, please!

9th December 2010

Do You Remember Me?

Do you know what hurts the most?
You don't even recognise me,
Have I turned to a ghost?
Have I turned to that forgotten memory rotting inside your head?
The one that screams, "I'm still alive, I am not dead!"
Do you remember me?
Have I become a figment of your imagination?
That thought that returns but you abruptly neglect
The one that haunts you and has a harrowing effect.

Do you remember the good times?
Yeah the ones we used to share
Back in the times when you used to care
Don't you hear the sound of my voice?
The one annoying your ears but it still lingers
Don't you hear me calling?
Don't you hear my whispers?

Do you feel my touch?
The one that used to heal.
Especially when you got caught
Just before you were about to steal.
Do you remember when I hit your face with my fist?
But it was by accident
Tell me do you still remember this?

Remember when money was what we used to spend
Just so we could go to school and start a new trend?

Do you remember when we said we'll last forever?
We'll never end...
Do you remember when I was your friend?

Do you remember the memories?
Do you remember me?

10th December 2010

Greed

The seed of greed is growing (clean)
If money is the root of all evil, then greed is the seed
Right now I'm overdosing on that seed
To feed the greed
Which makes me crave for the things I want and need
Even if it means people have to bleed.

11th December 2010

The Struggle Between Dreams and Reality

What if my dreams could become reality?
And I could transcend the mental barriers that separate the two worlds.
Because my dreams are a succession of images that illuminate my mind
They are the stars that shine in the dark midnight sky which is my mind
But I can only dream when I'm asleep.

Why can't my dreams affiliate with reality?
Taking away the unnecessary stress that your soul feels
Or subjugating the cold hate that makes your heart chill
Stripping you from the grief that is killing you
Soothe the frustration that tampers with your feelings
What if my dreams could be healing?
Easing the pain that torments your soul.

What if my dreams were your cure?
The cure to all the cynicism that plagues reality
The medicine for making you smile whilst you are surrounded by...
Hatred
I could fix it, I know my dreams can
But I have to find a way where I can
Knock down barriers.
My dreams are slaves whilst reality is the slave master,
Who continues to emasculate my dreams for the chance of freedom
But will it ever have the opportunity?

I dream dreams my dreams could never dream.
It is confusing but it will definitely free
The mental slavery

Reality has brought on you and me.
Can't you hear the screams of my dreams?
Or is reality making you deaf?
Making you disown the thing that can assuage your pain
I'm trying my hardest to show my dreams
But reality always seems to be in the way.

I cannot let my dreams be wasted.

But the terrible thing involved in reality
Won't let my dreams penetrate through.
So they are stuck.
Stuck in the back of my cranium
Waiting for me to dream again.
Waiting for the chance to drift and bring peace to humanity.
But I can only dream for this to happen.

Funny how I can dream in reality
But never get the chance for my dreams to be reality.
This unfair doing is degrading my dreams
Stripping them away from their duty.
I wish I could share my dreams with you
But they are stuck and reality won't let them through

What if my dreams could become reality?
And I could transcend the mental barriers that separate the two worlds?

11th December 2010

She Gave Her Heart Away Too Many Times

She gave her heart away too many times
She made her ears listen to too many lies
Her eyes saw what he was doing
But she was too in love.
Eyes became blind pain
Even though she's had enough
She was sick and tired of being sick and tired
Her mind wanted to leave this compulsive liar
But her heart couldn't
It kept saying 'no you shouldn't'
You still love him

She stayed with him
Now she has deteriorated
Every second with her lover she now hated
Her beauty was lost, she could never get it back
Now she looks back when she had the chance to leave
But all she does is cry and grieve
She still stays with him
She has now become a victim
To love.
She's had enough but can't leave
Because he has her heart
She is now dying from love
Although she doesn't know it
She will never be lonely but she will die a perilous death
Because love is killing her slowly
Every time she takes a breath.

12th of December 2010

Missing Grandad

I say a prayer for you at night
I even seem to write some lyrics for you near the candlelight
I wish I could see your white teeth shine so bright
But you're gone and I would like
To reminisce on the good times
I guess that seems alright
But it's hard to see those images since you're out of sight
Damn man, it's like I've seen a ghost
Because I keep having a fright
It feels like your right by my side
Oh how I miss the way you used to hug me tight

So here I am writing lyrics about you near candlelight
I gaze at the stars twinkling in the sky at midnight
They look just like your white teeth that used to shine so bright
I'm trying my hardest to write the things I liked
But I can't see without you, you were my sight
Please come back; come back when the time is right

13th of December 2010

I Just Want to Kiss You

I cannot.
Continue living like this.
Waiting, waiting for you
Just for a kiss
Break the vicious tension.
Kill the
Stuttering.
Gaze into my eyes.
Let them drift you away.
Stop thinking and
Just let me,
Kiss you.
That's all I want to do
I just want to kiss you.

14th December 2010

Poetry Saves

The darkness she was writing swallowed the light
Her heart sank lower, as she wrote the words on her mind
Scribbling and rushing, scared there wasn't enough time
This was her getaway, from all her pain.
When her pen touched the paper
It wrote down her memories
The ones she could remember
The ones she had seen but no one else knew
The memories you throw away
But she can't because they are stained
A stain that will last forever, but she had found a saviour
Something that took away her misery and agony
Something as beautiful as her
Her saviour was poetry

14th December 2010

No Hope

My brothers have no hope
And you wonder why we don't vote
If we vote, there will never be any change
We'll still be hurt, dying from the pain
Bullets will still be piercing through brains
I remember when I was an infant
So young and innocent,
But now I'm locked up in the system
My life could be stopped in an instant.
The government said things will change
But the deaths are still rising
So loving mothers are still crying
And yet the government are not realising
What is happening?
Tell me please, what is happening
I can't continue
Especially when the government don't realise the issue
They say change is good but when will it happen
When will the roads be safe?
When will young people stop sleeping in graves?
When will things change?
Damn, London needs to see change

15th December 2010

Angel of Death

The silhouette of my shadow is creeping up on me
Showing me time is of the essence
I can feel her presence
The angel of death
She is waiting to strike.
I shall die before my time
I shall die due to my beliefs
But can I be saved or am I in too deep
Time is running out
And my Shadow is getting closer
There is no time for me to cry
Because we are all destined to die
I don't know when I'll exhale my last breath
But am I ready for my untimely death?

18th December 2010

Starvation on Christmas Day

He lays there nonchalantly.
Belly bloated but it's not because he's had a good meal.
Far from it, he's malnourished.
Lucky to get a bread crumb
He looks up at his mum with starvation etched on his eyes.
But food plagues his mind
But what can she do?
She's in the same predicament too.
Very thankful for food when she gets it.
But she is never selfish
She shares it with her two-year-old boy
Who looks nine months pregnant.
How can this happen when I have more food than I need?
I eat more than seven plates to feed my greed
But he lays there, his tongue as dry as the sand he lays upon.
Sometimes he suckles AID infested milk, from his mum.

As I sit here this Christmas
Surrounded by all this lovely food on the table
I wonder if that little boy is able to survive.
I got all this delicious food around me
I even got another present from my mum
That boy is lying there naked and homeless
Lucky if he and his mum can find another bread crumb.

My heart goes out to him
His mother isn't incompetent
But she can't do anything

So her heart is broken.

She looks at her son's stomach; it's swollen.

You may have a good turkey

But he has malnourishment

Please try to acknowledge him

Because he may die this Christmas.

25th December 2010

That Somebody

There is always somebody who will hurt you
There will always be somebody that stains your mind
Every second of the day you take time to think of that somebody.
You want to free your love for that somebody.
Although that somebody is destined to hurt you
They never mean to because their love is true.
That somebody is worth all the pain
And that somebody is worth all the suffering
That somebody is worth all your loving.
Because that somebody just wants to love you
That somebody knows life is precious
They know it holds immense value
That is why they want to spend it with you
I know you've been hurt and you're feeling lonely.
I know you doubt trust but you can trust me
Please let me love you
I can be that somebody.

29th December 2010

The Personality of My Pen

I sit here and write what's on my mind
Hoping that you'll find time to figure out what plagues my life.
I'm writing to release all the pain and grief
It seems to be my only release.
A lot of people read my words
And realise my eyes always vilify the lies and promote the truth.
I just hope you can emphasise with me before I die
I tried to hide but being unrecognised hurts inside.
I don't mind if I'm not meant to be famous
Just as long as you remember me
I just don't want to die nameless.

Some people may call me an intellectual
I'm just a perpetual poet but only a few people know it
I think I should show it more often.
Because these words seem to soften my misery.
I seem to be a mystery, an enigma.
A confusing figure.
And that is the reason I write
Just for me to bring a message from my heart
Before I depart from this dark world.

So you can understand my emotions; so you can understand me
I don't mean to write; my pen has a mind of its own
And it seems to drift away slowly every time I'm alone.

30th December 2010

I Wonder if Heaven Has a Ghetto

I wonder if heaven has a ghetto
I mean a place for those youths who murdered and stole
Who lived on the streets whilst the rain was pouring down
Those boys who messed around
Because their fathers were never around.
Does heaven have a place for them?
Somewhere they can stay and relax
Even though they have stab wounds in their backs
Even though they sold marijuana to look after their mama's
I wonder if heaven has a ghetto.
I wonder if heaven has a ghetto
A place for those people stricken by poverty
Where their mothers don't have to struggle with a 9-to-5
Just so their baby's stomachs have food inside
A place where mothers don't have to raise children on their own
So they do not become a part of the single mother syndrome
I wonder if heaven has a ghetto.
I wonder if heaven has a ghetto
Where those girls don't have to sell their bodies
To get appreciation from men
Where they can be treated like young women
But not to the point where they are having children
A place for them to be surrounded by truth
And enjoy the precious days of their youth.
I wonder if heaven has a ghetto.

I wonder if heaven has a ghetto
Where men can take responsibility for their kids
Erasing all the bad things they have done
A place for them to be dads again
Can this only happen when
Heaven has a ghetto.

I wonder if heaven has a ghetto
I mean a place for those youths who murdered and stole.
Or for those fathers who were never there
And those girls who prostitute themselves just to feel like people care
A place for those mothers who struggled with a nine to five
Just for their children to stay alive.
I wonder if heaven has a ghetto

Undated 2010

Street Daddy

My bruddas are on these streets,
They ain't in pen but they need a release
From all the hate and agony,
Cos their dads weren't a part of the family.
So now the roadside's become their new daddy.
Not the type of dad to give love and fun,
He's the type of dad to give blood and a gun.
Type of dad that will lead you astray.
Or worse, leave you dead for your body to decay.

Undated 2010

An Enigma

My heart overflows with pain but only God knows
My pain is locked within, only my smile shows
So I am living a life you could say that's not me
I don't have to reveal my darkest secrets to you
So if you are offended I don't really care
Because I've done my job; yeah go-ahead and stare
I was born controversially so I'll die the same way
My days are numbered so that is why I pray
And thank Jah for my life and the years gone by
Even if some of the years I did cry, I won't lie
My belligerent, malignant pugnacious attitude to authority
Will either kill me or get me killed
And this is why my secrets are never revealed
Because where is the trust that Jah bestowed in people
It's gone so the people have turned evil
And I'm here speaking truth and they don't want to listen
But if I told them lies you'll see their eyes glisten
So I shall forever stay as that enigma
That confusing but mysterious figure; named Alexander (HA-HA)

Undated 2010

Don't Get Too Close to Me

Don't get too close to me, I have a lot of issues.
I hold my tears, so I have no use for tissues
But use of love, misuse and one fatal excuse I have left my pride bruised
And my pain continues.
I don't trust you, I don't even trust myself,
I want to and I know I need your help
But I feel so paranoid
Plus, my foolish ego seems to avoid trusting you,
So I fall in a void where I see a dark abyss
And when I see the sunshine
The moon takes the piss and blocks it,
So all I see is an eclipse.
I'm lost and I'm not sure I want to be found
I had a girl who lifted me up when my spirit was down
Will I ever find that again before they bury me in the ground?
Sometimes I dislike my friends because they betray me
Sometimes I dislike like myself because I see the worst in me
But when I see the best of me the rest of me is filled with jealousy

My mother keeps on telling me, keep praying
And I still do but only because it's a routine
Do I still believe? I still dream about him
But If God is the Father why hasn't he paid a visit?
I don't even want to swear or get explicit
I'm just angry and confused.
I made a vow to my mother that I'll be modest
But let's be honest, tomorrow is not promised
So I'll still be continuing my egotistical nonsense

Should I care for my friends if they don't care for me?
I know some fake friends that have turned into real enemies
And I know I will never hurt them, I will always love them
But I love my life too much to be in the company of them
Is it wrong if I don't accompany them?

Undated 2010

My Generation

These streets are where we grew up
And unfortunately where some of us die.
Mother's hearts break and they cry
They can't bear the heartache and ask God why?
Why is life so wrong, why are the youth like this?
We're in an unstable condition, we need help
Cos we're in a crisis
We're not living, we are just existing
I reminisce on when I was an infant
But now I live in reality
And my life could be taken in an instant.
I just pray for better times, I pray for an easier life
I talk but no one listens
So I seem to write.
Too many people have died in the past years
I don't cry, I don't shed any tears
Not because I'm heartless and I don't care
But what's the point if another brother
Has a much harder life somewhere?
Just know that they remain in my heart
They may be gone but the love never departs
There are too many to name
All were innocent even if some were in the 'game'
I just hope and pray you are easy and relaxing
Smiling and enjoying your time in God's mansion.
And it's hard living without you
But we got to keep moving on
We've been hurt for too long

Now it's time to be strong cos life goes on.
Even though you're dead, memories we've shared
Are always in our heads.
You mums have lost a child, things have gone wild
Now it been a while since I flashed a true smile.
The governments say we're going through a phase
This has made a couple people rage
And my heart and blood spills on this page
There's some yutes out there who know
More yutes dead than their current age
This generation is moving kinda strange.
And now I'm thinking to myself, will shit ever change?
R.I.P my bruddas

2nd January 2011

An Outsider

Sometimes I feel like I'm an outsider
An alien stranded on foreign lands
I pour out my heart and my love and I get neglected
This has affected me; it seems no one understands me
Maybe I am living a fantasy
But how can this be if I'm among people in reality?
I just want you to understand me
I'm a popular guy
So why do I feel so lonely?

3rd January 2011

Let Me Die a Happy Man

I hope I spark the flame of a brain to make a change.
I just want to be a comforter, let me assuage your pain,
Let me ease your mind so you can forget about the blood stains
That leave an imprint on the floor.
If I can be the reason you leave your front door
With your teeth shining ready to smile
And your heart innocent like a little child.
If I can do that then I am proud
Then I will be ready for God to take me up to the clouds.

If I can make you addicted to love
Instead of drugs
The ones that circle your environment.

If my words could be encouragement, to a broken youth
And highlight the truth.
So you won't have to lie to friends.
I wish I could make a change before I die;
The type of change that'll make me feel good inside.
Soothe the pain of the darkest heart
And take away the emotional scars and let the pain depart.
I will die happy, getting rid of my misery,
If I could just shower you with love, just enough
To ease the pain and calm the rain.

If I could do all of this
I would die in bliss.
If I could just make you smile,
I would die a happy man
If I could just make you love
I would die a happy man.

3rd January 2011

The Struggle to Live

Staying alive is easier than living.
Taking is so much easier than giving.
That's why it's so easy to become depressed
When you are living the life of one who is oppressed.
Especially when they take away what is yours.
Be smart whilst being rebellious
You don't have to break laws to open doors.
I suggest you use your senses
Instead of becoming senseless.
Do not have a lack of awareness
Can't you see the system is never at rest?
Loads of people are feeling oppressed
But what are you gonna do about this?

Seize the opportunities you have
Never let go of your dreams
May the tears you once cried produce streams
That will eventually turn into oceans.
Set your aspirations into motion.
You don't have to be another number calculated in this system.
Because taking is easier than giving,
And staying alive is easier than living.
So it's better to start living rather than existing.

9th January 2011

The Place Where Danger Waits

I go to the place where danger waits
I associate but I know it's bound to forsake me.
The fear caged inside of me
Screams aloud but you don't hear it.
When I stroll there, I casually swallow spit
I've noticed this has left an imprint on the way I think.
So stupid minded, why did I chose this route?
So foolish, now I'm stuck in a loop
An eternal spiral, I cannot leave
But this is my fault.
This terror burns like a wound
Being tormented by granules of salt.

I see the harrowing images that take away my breath.
I have foreseen my own death,
This has forced me to tread carefully.
I am forever paranoid; I don't trust no noise.
I try to avoid any contact with this place
But it waits for me to make a mistake.
It consumes the presence of my fear
Although surrounded by darkness the outcome is clear.
Here in his place is where my end is near.

A lonesome figure is who I am.
Because this place does not permit the company of man.
Lost in a place you will not find,
A place you cannot find
Alone but the time ticking away comforts me

A plague of irony takes place.
Because the time wasted is closer to the time where
I come face to face with my fate.
Although I have seen my death, I don't appreciate it.
Tied together but I do not want to commit
Located in a scary place where danger waits
Where I half-heartedly associate but the most terrifying thing is
My death stares straight into my face.

9th January 2011

Looking Up at the Sky

The clear blue sky
Along with the bright sun shine.
A combination that deserves appreciation
But gets taken for granted
I don't know why

The lost sheep go wandering around
Looking for a place to settle down.
They move nonchalantly,
Just lost travellers
But they never make a sound.

I look up and gaze
At the clouds moving in different ways.
The azure of the sky.
The beautiful light of the sun.
For this, God surely deserves some praise.

10th January 2011

Just Writing For the People

Just writing, I'm just writing.
I'm not writing just for myself
I'm writing for the pensioners with bad health
Who are tired and lonely
But seems no one recognises their wealth.

I'm just writing for the deceased
The young and the old
The one's who smiled with joy
Or the ones who suffered with grief.
I say a prayer for you every day.
Just to make sure you are okay.
Grandad I miss you, even though you're dead and gone
But I write so your memory lives on.

I'm just writing for the people of the streets.
Some of them trapped in the ghetto.
May you take opportunities so you can let go
Of the harsh situations you find yourself in
Just because you sin
It doesn't mean I should be judging
Because we are all the same
Just different due to our outlook on pain.

This is for the oppressed who feel broken hearted.
Close to being depressed because their dreams haven't started
Keep your head up.
I know it seems tough but hopefully you'll make it
Knowing that you have my love.

I write for all the mothers
Who struggle with a nine to five
Just to make sure their children stay alive.
I want to thank you for your patience
Soon your turmoil will rot away
Because your grateful children will make you smile one day.

I write for the fathers
Who treat their daughters like princesses and
Teach their sons how to be a man.
I want to say thank you
Cos you do the best you can.

You see I write for the people and not just me.
I also write for the prisoners located in captivity
Because I believe you are not evil
You just couldn't cope.
But don't worry you are still people
Because you still believe in hope
I just write for the people
Especially the ones made to struggle.

11th January 2011

Oh What a Beautiful Day

Oh gosh
I must be lost in happiness
Because I seem to squash the sadness
I did.
Each eyelid that covers my eyes
Is getting kissed by the autumn breeze
No surprise as to why my mind is in ease.
It's resting in peace, although it isn't dead
So now my head is oozing with positivity
And my mouth ejaculates words that despise negativity.
Can't you see even my mama is proud of me?
The blue sky just cleanses my soul
And it just seems to revolve itself in joy.
I'm feeling innocent just like a little boy
Oh what a beautiful day.
Can't you see the elegant birds have come out to play?
I know this happiness is bound to stay
I just know I will show
My beautiful smile
Tomorrow.

12th January 2011

Impatient Love Losing Patience

Yes, my love is undying
And no, I am not denying
The fact that I love you.
I just can't wait for you.
Do you think I am destined
To see tomorrow?
If I was, I would wait a thousand years
No questions,
Cos you're the reason I have no sorrow.
But during those years I will shed a million tears
Because you are not next to me.
But I cannot cage my love
It needs to be free.
I do not want to wait
Even if that means you're not with me.

12th January 2011

The Hurt Soldier

I'm a soldier but nobody fights with me
But everybody puts their misery on top of my shoulders
As I grow older simultaneously my heart gets colder
All by myself to fight these battles
Enclosed in a small corner.
But I guess this is how life goes
People have told me to stop being miserable
But they continue to bestow their pain
Onto my soul, so I fall
In a state of feeling low.

The gun of pain shoots bullets into my heart
As I continue to walk in this battlefield
And my only shield is my word
That seems to conceal how I feel.
Although I'm scared I don't show it
Although it hurts, you will never know it
Because I'm a soldier who tries his best
And although I wear a bullet proof vest
There's still blood stains on my chest.
But I live to see a next battle.

12th January 2011

Hoping To See Better Days

I see destruction coming in different ways
But still I remain hopeful
Hoping to see better days.
Longing to hear laughter of the children
Or hear the loud voice of an evangelical pastor.
Surrounded by darkness but light will soon penetrate
And eradicate all the hate.
But until that day, I continue to pray
Hoping for better days.

13th January 2011

My Sister

Where do I start?
You have half my blood but the whole of my heart
You will forever play a big part in this drama
That I call life.
Don't you see you make me calmer?
You seem to drain all this pain and strife.
This soul loves you and will protect you
Walk the corners of this earth for you if you want me to.

You don't need more blood to fill any gap
Because your personality handles that
It erases the fact that we may not be blood
But this heart seems to beat enough blood
Filled with unconditional love
Dedicated for you
Hopefully you know it's true.

There are times you agitate me
Frustrate me, sometimes you aggravate me
But I won't let that spoil this poem,
You see
Because you look after me and Lamarr
The love we have for you is symbolised
As the brightest star.
At the end of its life it will have an explosion
But only to signify our love and devotion.
Do not forget Lamarr, he may stay quiet
But his love for you is never silent.

Half of my blood but the whole of my heart
The love caged in me and Lamarr will never depart
Can you imagine that?
You should feel happy too
Cos you got some sexy black brothers, lovin' you.

13th January 2011

Save the Children

Save the children, preserve their innocence.
The future of humanity relies on them.
An amazing creation; the beautiful children.
Watch them gracefully play
So carefree to the pain.
Just oblivious to everything apart from smiling.
Oh, when they smile doesn't your heart skip a beat?
When you hear their laughter don't you feel warm inside?
But when you see them cry,
Don't you just want to die?

Save the children and love them
Make them feel special and unique
Because they help you through your hardest trials
Especially when they smile.
Save the children because they make life worthwhile.

15th January 2011

Just Recognise My Love, Please

I could never deny you of my love,
That's why it isn't a secret.
Although you don't feel the same, please keep it.
I'd rather you knew my love
Than my love be a stranger.
My love is too deep so my emotions drown
There's a sense of danger
But I suffocate whenever you're not around.
Why don't you feel the same?
Please try to replicate my love
Instead of making my heart die in pain
My love is more than enough for you.
Love is a precious thing that you should cherish
But why do you constantly want it to perish?

I want you to want me.
Because this is getting ridiculous
You continue to remain oblivious
To my love
Why do you do this?
Whilst I sit here craving for a kiss,
A touch.
But my heart is dying
Cos you don't recognise my love.

15th January 2011

In Love With Life

No need to consume negative vibes
Cos I'm still alive
Although I'm still trying to survive
I'm in love with life;
The beautiful women who pass me by
And the righteous men who walk with pride,
They influence my young life.
My eyes look up at the sky and I thank God
Cos I've been through a lot
But I never stop having love for life.

Yesterday I had the darkest night
And today I will have a brighter day
Because my love for life is here to stay
And everything seems to be alright.
Damn, I love life.
I'm so happy to be alive.

17th January 2011

Inherited Sufferings

Reminiscing on the days when kissin'
Was what couples used to do
Now they're in a position where they only seem to argue.
Broken vows; what happened to "for better or for worse"?
Now people have forgotten love and that hurts
Especially when they have kids
So their kids' hearts split.
Loyalty is the question that parents are asking
Leading kids to depression that makes their hearts sink.
Can't believe this is happening to mum and dad
The kids suffer to a point beyond being sad
Some have got used to the pain, others suffer in silence
But they can't tell no one, there's no guidance.
So now they're in the middle of a divorce
Are they hurting inside?
Of course!

17th January 2011

So Paranoid

Have you ever felt so paranoid that you don't trust your own boys?
Trapped in a cage where your brain questions itself
Asking whether it has mental health issues.
So you don't trust people but yet you're a person
Trying to trust yourself but it ain't working
You're still hurting
Mother's still concerned and she's yearning
For you to change.
But you can't cos you're stuck in an element,
Your mind still holds relevance.
Imagine paranoia is a house and you're its resident
I constantly think 'will I give this to a descendant
Am I a product of my environment'?

Turning my neck so fast I get whiplash
Itching my skin as if I have a rash.
Dark shadows follow you in the light
And the bright moon follows you at night
You want to stay inside and clear your mind
But I can't confide in myself.
People fight wars with people whilst
I fight wars with myself, no one else.
I prayed to God but I can't see him
It must be a sin to be paranoid
Cos you don't trust the love people show
Too scared to tell people what you go through
Same day but ain't nothing new
Going through hell, so you feel you're hell proof

But the truth is
You're paranoid and you don't trust your boys
Too scared to show yourself, so nobody is a witness.

18th January 2011

Love Is a Battlefield

Love is a battlefield.
Where you run the risk of getting shot by cupid
There is no time for being stupid, you may die from it.
But it is worth it
The medal you gain is your opponent's heart
Blood, sweat and tears occur from the start.
But it is worth it
The sweet victory is perfect.

After you die you will still be alive
Remembered with pride.
Your battle was necessary for your name to survive
Now everyone shall live in your legacy because you tried
And succeeded in this battle.

Your victory will be remembered wherever you are
For both of you have made history amongst the stars.
Even when you die
Your love will remain alive.
As for me, I am still fighting
I am not denying
That it is hard to handle
This heart breaking battle.
But although I'm forced to suffer
This battle is worth it
Just to be with my victorious lover.

18th January 2011

Floating Memories

When I die please don't cry
Just remember me.
I'll still be around
To make sure you're safe and sound.
Just reflect on the good times and the memories we shared
They won't be hard to find and I also will be there.
The place you keep your memories
Is the place you'll see my face:
I'm still alive with the memories you'll find
Floating in your mind

18th January 2011

Dreams Can Produce Anything

We can fly high like those helium balloons
That reach for the sky
Or maybe we can make dreams flow like streams.
Our obstacles can become mountains
If we don't amount to nothing
But we can shoot aspirations like
Water from fountains.
Instead of becoming stars
Why don't we live amongst the stars?
In the midnight blanket?
Just think about it
Paint pretty pictures that only our souls can see
Let us create a legacy or maybe a dynasty
Raise kings and queens;
Let hope be the castle that we live in
And our crowns can be dignity.

Let love be the language we speak
And let care be the actions we show.
We can be angels who carry a glow and a halo.
Let us be the sunshine when it rains
Let the sunshine erase our pain.
We can be anything.
We can be kings and queens
If we continue to dream.

20th January 2011

Yesterday

Yesterday, I will never get to see you again
So long my friend but to not worry
I will remember you with my pen
I reminisce on the time you made me smile
My eyes overflowing with tears of joy.
Thank you for your kindness even if it's in the past
Memories we shared will always seem to last.
But now I have to say hello to today
And then hope and pray I see tomorrow
Hopefully, you know you took away my sorrow.

21st January 2011

Let Us Dance Under the Moonlight

We don't have enough money to go to the clubs
But we have each other and we have love.
No dancing shoes but we have our feet
Let them move to the rhythm of our heartbeats.
Let's go outside and dance in the garden
Let our feet soften the pain
Let us dance under the stars in the sky
Let us dance.
Let us dance under the moonlight.

21st January 2011

Abusing Love

Maybe we were too young
Two ignorant, innocent youths abusing love
Abusing trust, abusing us.
We didn't understand our feelings
Our hearts were bleeding because of our conflicting emotions.
Restricting each other's devotion with our hate filled words
We didn't understand love
We just continued to hurt one another
You were a turbulent lover but so was I
As time went by we couldn't understand why
We kept on running back to each other.
Continuously forced to suffer
We hated but yet we loved
But was it real love?
We had enough but why didn't we leave?
I never received love
And we never seemed to commit
Always cheating and deceiving
But too scared to split.

Stupid decisions cemented with different reasons
Stayed through the rain in different seasons
Why did we put ourselves through this?
Too scared to split and too scared to love
We had a hate filled relationship
And even though we had enough, we came back for more.
Continually making our abused hearts sore.

23rd January 2011

Do You Have a Heart to Spare?

A young girl smiles but she cries from the inside
She needs a heart so I want to give her mine
She's dying but values life.
But nobody seems to help
She needs a donor
But everybody wants to disown her.
She needs closure; peace of mind
But she can't find the time
As she lays there dying
She's constantly trying
To produce enough blood to sustain her.
Family showers her with love to maintain her
Tried to give blood but each one was a failure.

She knows there is a person out there
Who can help her,
But who really cares, who is willing to try?
To save this young girl who is destined to die
She patiently waits for applicants on the donor list
To present her with a gift
A gift of life, a gift to live
But who is willing to give that gift?

It seems like society
Forgets the people who are forced to suffer silently
That young girl probably wants to cry herself to sleep
Longing for someone to help her.
She needs a heart
But do you have enough heart to save her?

25th January 2011

My Family, The Heavenly Souls

Heavenly souls who graciously stroll this earth
With loving personalities that will melt the coldest heart
This love for them is never to depart
An unconditional, spiritual love
That one may never experience.

Beautiful masterpieces created from the artistic hands of God
They will never understand this love
My affection burns like an eternal candle
It may be too much to handle
But it will never end.
This love will transcend all barriers
It will create dreams into reality.
I am surrounded by beautiful souls
I thank God for my family.

26th January 2011

No Army and Squad; Just Myself and My Beautiful God

What have I done to deserve this?
Constantly forced to feel worthless
Although I am not perfect
What have I done to deserve this?

Where associates at school question my sanity
Forever doubting my mind's clarity.
Surrounded by people I do not trust
But seem to love
Ironic how I never see that love return
So my singed heart is forced to burn
In a continual flame that one's eyes could never see
But their souls could feel and their loving words could heal.
But they do not witness and they do not see
Forcing them to question my sanity
And asking what is really wrong with me?

Trapped in a cycle
Trying to come out but I'm stuck
But I guess it is my fault.
Who will be the next victim in this sickening system?
Consumed by adult themes
But yet, were still children.

But why do I moan and why do I curse?
Because I have you and your words seem to be true
You always guide me even through the weaves that leave me tangled
Affiliated with thieves and sin and I admit to being strangled

But your care, your trust and your love; that is more than enough
I can feel your presence even though we never physically touch.
We are spiritually connected
Oxygen caresses my lungs but you leave me breathless
And although I move reckless
I could never be stressed
I am too blessed
I guess you seem to test me but I am ready.

I am ready to walk this journey
Even if it means to be alone
I will give up my pride, greed and my own home.
I am on my own; no army and no squad
No knives and no guns
Just happiness and true love.
No army and no squad
Just myself and my beautiful God!

3rd February 2011

Runaway From This Fiery Cauldron

Why is it always me to kill my aspirations?
I want to be free but I'm caged in
Roaming the fearsome roads of anger
A sense of danger.
A shadow of my former self; I've become stranger.
You don't recognise me and I don't recognise myself
Disgusted by what I see in the mirror
And yeah I'm getting bigger but this soul is getting smaller.
This world is getting colder, so I'm getting hotter
So my mind's a black cauldron of fire
And it produces these flammable words
The fire is unbearable and my mind hurts

It feels like my brain's got a haemorrhage
These aggressive words and thoughts cause damage
I guess I'm a slave to my talent
But I can't overcome this challenge
These thoughts are hard to manage and hard to maintain
My mind's vision is deluded by the pleasurable pain.
I know this pain and anger is not here to stay
But will I see tomorrow or should I start today?
The answer to my problems
RUNAWAY!

4th February 2011

Young Black Brothers

Perpetually patrolling with paranoid people
Although paranoid they contradict their ways
And show the type of tenacious trust towards others.
They have dazzling dreams and amazing aspirations
But surreptitiously get stuck in sickening sin.
Crawling with pride like the black panthers
Rising from the gutter, not related but they are my brothers
Who continue to share love for each other
They spread love but yet forced to suffer
This is dedicated to all my young black brothers
Stuck in a spiralling system.
Keep ya head up!
Throw away your harrowing hate and spread love.

5th February 2011

Restricting My Dream of Success

I seem to deviate from my potential
This may be consequential
Producing a negative outcome
And now my heart is numb
My conscience is conscious of my foolish decisions
I am in a competition with myself
I have dreams of living happily
But will this ever happen if I affiliate with apathy?
I am naturally blessed, I guess
But I never put no effort to overcome life's tests.

I could never emulate the success of other greats
I refuse to imitate because that would violate my inner being
I refuse to conform to normality
So I am okay if people don't understand me
Because I don't understand myself:
Constantly fighting wars with myself
Restricting my dreams that should move mountains
But they gain dust on a hopeless shelf

Am I a star who should shine brightly in the sky?
I haven't reached my peak because I'm scared of heights
But I'm not afraid to die
So why do I dodge my destiny?
Maybe some things in life are meant to be

6th February 2011

There's Enough Hope to Change

He was never in allegiance with gentleman
He half-heartedly strolled with drug dealers and fake friends
Thieves, fiends, and a company of sinful beings
Who did illicit deeds
But he didn't like the roads
Constantly committing crime missing his real friends
Because they're currently doing time
Surrounded by thieves and fiends
But he has dreams.
There's enough hope to change!

She was used and abused
Heartless boys left her confused
Her body was misused.
Heartless girls always judge her
No one seems to love her
The pain of rain falls in the sunniest weather
Does she have to feel this way forever?
There's enough hope to change!

She's gonna lose her job
She is struggling to pay the bills
Alone at night, she talks to God
Hoping He'll help her through
What is she supposed to do?
Her kids need clothes and food
But what is she to do?
There's enough hope to change!

He's a slave to mental chains
Looking for freedom but he doesn't think things will be the same.
He is his own enemy seeming to inflict pain
All his bad memories seem to drain
His positivity.
Optimism is a false hope, a cult religion
Tormented from his own vision
Leading to mental strains
But
There's enough hope to change!

We may not be in the best position
But there is no time for intermissions
Time to complete our missions constructed by intelligent decisions
There's enough help to change!

No matter where you come from
And no matter what you have done
Even if sorrow hurts you, you are not cursed
And although our souls harbour pain
There is enough hope to change!

7th February 2011

The Lonely Nomad in the Harshest Deserts

Walking through the harshest deserts.
Regardless of these shooting arrows;
I'm their target but they seem to be harmless
The sun beats on my back,
I'm like a camel but instead of sitting fat,
I'm storing memories just remember that,
Terrified of what the future may hold,
I've seen dreams more precious than gold.
I possess stories that have been left untold,
Although I carry these I have no home.
Just a lonely nomad, walking the desolate path of no man's land;
Nobody to hold my hand.
I'm walking through these deserts, surrounded by dust and sand
That are consuming my legs, my legs refusing instructions from my head
Sand grains everywhere; trying to make me sink.
Obscuring my vision, so I choose not to blink.
Foolish decisions, why didn't I care to think.
My throat's dry and sore; I need a drink.
So I'm dehydrated, but these words still pour
And leave murky puddles on the floor.
No trustworthy instruments, so I write with a stick.
Paranoid it's poison so I'm afraid of ink,
Carried with prepared poise, so I suspect
The unexpected noise.
Forced to grow old, no longer a boy, no need for innocent toys.

Oh, what a madness
Surrounded by silence but still hear echoes of sadness.

Blinded by rage but I still see shadows of pain.

A montage of images, I see a mirage of false hope

It's so damn sickening but right now I'm sinking in.

I'm sinking into the crowd of sand,

No shade but I'm stuck with these shadows.

Not a hanged man but my head is hanging low

The sun spirals silently, my mind is spinning violently, my heart is hurting.

I wish I could go inside and see.

My feet are hurting but this pen won't let me be.

One cactus gets repeated so it turns into cacti.

Surrounded by annoying fires and bloodthirsty mites,

I try with all my might to ignore them

But I'm agitated by their bites;

Trapped in the twirling turns of confusion.

Just an illusion whilst this dirty sandstorm carries pollution.

The sunlight intertwines with the moon so I guess it's an eclipse.

But it's getting overshadowed and I fall into a dark abyss.

This brown skin has been burnt to a singe

A metaphorical door for hope has no door hinge but I continue to run;

Too ignorant to learn, so this abused back is made to burn.

In this desert I am trapped but I yearn to go back and not be a nomad.

I want to be accepted in my home town but I'm now a grown man.

Just a lonely nomad stuck in recurring spirals of sandstorms

That occur in no man's land.

11th February 2011

Would You Do the Same? Would You?

If I died tonight would you cry?
If I went to prison would you visit me?
Would you try and write?
If you saw my eyes cry, would you console me?
Would you hold me?
Would you?

All those things mentioned I would do
This question brings so much pain but would you do the same?
Would you?

11th February 2011

Time Ticks Away So Slowly

Time
Ticks away so
Slowly.
Praying
I haven't reached the time for my soul to
Sleep.
Laying
Lazily on the concrete floor;
Tired.
But
My eyes forever stare at the punishing
Clock.
Not
Too long before the fun
Stops.

Time
Ticks away so
Slowly.
Do
I have enough time to stop myself feeling so
Lonely?

14th February 2011

Destiny Better be Good To Me

Destiny better be good to me
Or I'll change her with lady Liberty.
I'm still flirting with Hope
Me and her spoke words.
She wants to take away all my hurt bones and feelings
And she is always revealing
Happiness to me, who gives me a sense of positivity and clarity.
I think I'm going to ask Miss Happiness to marry me.
Maybe we can plant seeds of joy
Make kings and queens: little girls and boys.

But I have this associate; Agony
Agony always angers me so I mingle with Apathy.
Apathy, she's a beautiful girl if you want to be lazy.
I got this one deceiver called Paranoia
Makes me believe everyone is after me and I'm filled with disgust
There's a lack of trust
So I'm missing love and Mrs Love is taken by everyone else.
Mrs Love is not finding me even though I'm screaming for help
But I'm soon going to make her mine; I just need more time.

So Destiny please be good with me
Do your best with me
And I swear you will set me free
Free to be me, free to live happily
Instead of free to be lonely.

16th February 2011

I Cried Last Night

I cried last night
The tears freely ran down my face
With no inhibitions.
Asserted in different positions
Each fitter in the right place
I was lonely and cold hoping for someone to hold me tight
But no one came to my rescue
Ignoring my harrowing cries
Is this the same treatment in the event of my demise?
No one to say 'can I help you'
No one was in sight.

I cried last night.

28th February 2011

Broken Promises

I'm tired of these broken promises that cement our broken future
This punctured heart is deflated and this tormented mind is demented
Of all the memories we've collected,
We selected to reminisce on the bad ones
I remember when our hearts desires
Were to shower each other with kisses
But those memories are missing
Distant fingers stuck in a hazy vision
Through our soul's intermissions our destiny collapsed
This self-harming love has relapsed
And there's no turning back

I know you feel the same pain I feel
Trapped in a fantasy game, but life is so real
All we seem to do is argue
Now I'm wondering are you
Used to the fact that we argue?
The same emotions revolving
The essence of pain is still patrolling
I'm in the same predicament as you.
Beating together in unison to the rhapsodies of failure
The lies are reflections of what is now true.
The look in your eyes is now killing me
It's like you are testing me
I want to spread this testimony
But there's nobody to console me
Body to hold me
I guess I'm cursed to be lonely until my soul sleeps

We led a life that was on one pathway

But it divided and we were forced to strain

And we decided to keep it that way

And now our tired souls harbour pain

And now our tired voices can't speak because we scream at each other

And now our arrogant hearts have turned weak.

Maybe we were doomed from the start?

Maybe this love was meant to depart?

The innocent smiles and laughs are no more

Replaced with cruel frowns and stares

I can't take this any more

But how can I live if you are not there?

Wrongful lovers who produce hate but it feels right

The night brings the harshest pain but so does the morning light

1st March 2011

Paranoid On a Late Night

It's a late night.
I should really be sleeping but the events
Of this evening have left me feeling paranoid.
I'm just alone with my thoughts
That try to fill this lonely void of space in my mind.
I can't find the time to unwind.
So here I am sitting in this lonely chair
Inhaling the coldest air; nobody's here
But I hear footsteps on the stairs.

It's funny how things change.
Friends start to act strangely, then they turn into enemies.
So now I'm analysing associates, thinking will they betray me.
Maybe I'm thinking too much, maybe I should sit back and laugh.
Reminisce on the good times, with good guys
Who once enhanced my good life.
Instead of being paranoid, tormented by the noise of sirens;
Visualising acts of violence, witnessing death approach
Greeted by the chill of cold silence.
I saw my brother die; I saw his mother cry.
Then I saw another, run away with a bloodied knife.

I'm paranoid but at least I'm safe.
Satisfied by the comfort of this chair,
Because there is nothing but madness and cruelness on the streets out there.
They will kill you and they don't care.

5th April 2011

The World is Sick

The world is sick.
Vomiting negativity, only to consume again
Then it becomes too paranoid to trust a friend.
Its hazy eyes have got it seeing double vision.
So crazy guys tell lies to promote division.
Its abused heart has been pumping hatred and spite
An insomniac; too afraid to dream at night,
So nightmares seem to wreak loose;
Murderous eyes stare at victims and some prey on the youth.
The earth seems to cough up the reddest blood
Whilst other planets look on in disgust.

This earth is growing old but is it growing wise?
Destined to be bold but instead growing lies.
The earth is excreting away happiness
But is constipated with sadness.
It lies around in filth and waste
Damaging its pure, gracious face,
Smoking and polluting; benefiting the cause of a disaster.
Succumbed to mental and physical pain but cannot find the answer.

Who will cure this sick world?
Where older men rape little girls.
Who will look after this sickly Earth?
After years of damage have degraded its worth
Who can find a cure?
To make this frail, gaunt Earth what it once was:
Pure.

8th April 2011

The Hawk

These restless eyes search for companionship;
I long for the day we can be friends.
But I am torn.
My stomach mourns itself to sleep but comes alive, when blood stains
The tip of my beak.
Forgive my actions; they are just poisonous tears
That I have not shed over the years.

Perpetually patrolling in the friendly sky;
I roam this kingdom with murderous talons.
I swoop over luscious clouds, gaze at my talent.
Inferior birds find this a challenge.
The white, metal birds soar amongst my territory cautiously
Forever watching my movement
With jealousy.

I timidly dodge bullets from devils below
But my heart is punctured, I am lonely.
I am isolated in my own fear
My beak squawks foolishly with false pride
Whilst my eyes glimmer with paranoia.
That I try to hide.

I am worthy.
Foolish lies do not hurt me.
My homicidal throat is thirsty for blood.
Alone; oblivious to the affections of love.
A wondrous king with tortured wings

I soar.

I soar until these gracious wings can't soar any more.

Pleasurable pain etched on my brain.

Just a flying paradox. A living contradiction.

But it is more important to survive than be content with extinction.

18th May 2011

The Garden of Eden: Forbidden Fruit and Flowers

When our love began, it bloomed like the daffodils of spring
So blissfully.
But now it has ended, like all great things but it ended miserably.
Such a beautiful love, we once shared
So vibrant and pure but bittersweet memories linger for
This love is no more.
Spoiled by lies that only our foolish brains would believe
Our naive eyes were made to be deceived.
Each rumour entered every room of our love but it never closed a single door.
So this relationship was vulnerable, visible to strangers
Our love has run its course, tired and aged,
Withering away from the intense heat of star-crossed lovers.
Nurtured by nature, nonchalantly; pain and pleasure.
With my misty eyes, I'm mystified by this mystery
I wonder if you are missing me.
The love died, scorched and burnt
Beautiful yet ugly; a paradoxical garden.
Lessons learnt, but scars still sting with a never ending hurt.

When our love ended, it withered away like a strangled thorn bush
In the peak of summer
So disastrously.
If only I could put the fruit back on the tree.

5th August 2011

Thieves

Thieves in the day
Thieves in the night
Some are stealing chains
Someone stealing cars
No care in the world, but they have skill
No care in the world so some may kill
Some work for the government
Some work for the police
Some work for themselves
No matter who they work for
They will rob
Rob drops of your pride and confidence
Rob you of your happiness and rights
Some will rob you off the of the seats on your bikes
They'll rob the rich and rob the poor
No mercy for any child, any woman
Any man, anyone.
Whether you are the wealthy doctor
Or the poorest whore

But the biggest thief is the one stealing souls.
You can't protect yourself, you have no control.

6th August 2011

Freedom or Free Doom

She's looking at the world in a different view, a different perspective.
Her brain is playing games with her, memories once collected
Are now thrown away and disrespected.
The word freedom corrupts her brain, whilst free doom drives her insane.
The word is beautiful; plentiful but has a different meaning
A sense of healing, a means of breathing.
Take it away from her and her body's forever sleeping.

She says they fear what they don't understand
And hate what they can't conquer.
They can't fathom a phantom; so they quiver in fear
Whilst they hate what doesn't shiver and quiver with fear
At the sight of them; these feeble minded men.
Tell a friend to hold contempt and respect for evil minded men.

Intelligence holds no relevance
Ever since we lost our innocence.
Our inner sense interacts with our never ending nonsense.
So even the fool can be the teacher, whilst the teacher plays the fool.
So the foolish will fool, whilst the thinkers of society
Will decrease and eventually fall.

Society is getting weaker she said;
The revolutionary speaker won't see change until he's dead.
They messed with her head, these words, these thoughts
They spread and freed doom until it bloomed like geraniums.
Her cranium won't be the same again, all because of the word:
Freedom.

Looking at the world in a different view
The simplest things seem complex
When they are staring right in front of you.

5th October 2011

Will I Rest in Peace or Rest in Pieces?

Will I rest in peace or rest in pieces?
My cousin suffers from those epileptic seizures
It's times like these where I feel I need Jesus
But it's times like these where I say Jesus needs us.
Will I die from greed or get stricken by different diseases?
But greed is the thing that feeds us.
I never want my future children to ask *why did daddy leave us?*
I'm just contemplating and concentrating on life
Will I live to see a wife or will my mum visit the morgue because her son died,
With wounds from the blade of a knife?
I'm thinking too much probably, but honestly
It'll be a blessing if I reach 25, because over 20 lives passed in this city of mine.

I'm still smiling because life is precious and I still own it.
I notice not a lot of people know this
So I'm grateful, but a lot of people are hateful.
I choose to think clearly and freely but I'm asking the Lord to free me
From my life of sin, from the strife within and I pray
If I'm blessed enough, my next of kin won't inherit the same thing.
I ask the same unanswered questions for different reasons
Will I rest in peace or rest in pieces?

8th November 2011

Speak Life

We talk life not death
We still think because it's not illegal yet.
We dream together; so we believe together
When dreams become reality we achieve together.
Let no eye cry for fear and sorrow
For we believe in a brighter tomorrow
And therefore better days are bound to follow
May our despair turn into hope.

We will replace war with peace
And hatred with the love.
We will stop living on our knees
And we will rise above the struggle,
The pain and all of life's troubles.
Negative words shall have no effect
When positive actions continue,
Happiness and laughter will solve any issue

We speak life until life no longer speaks to us
For better days shall follow today
And tomorrow will have an easier pathway
Good over evil, love over hatred
And life over death.
Forever laughing until our last breath

10th November 2011

Six Feet Under

Now I know they say, I'm supposed to bury you in the grave
But I'd rather decay living and breathing,
Than have an honest reason to put my heart through that pain
If you died before me, tears would fall like leaves in the autumn season
And my nose would be sneezing
Whilst my cold heart will leave my chest freezing.
I love you, you're the one who was there for me.
You're the one who cared for me
Even when society was the one that stood and stared at me, sneered at me
It would be a tragedy, a travesty, if you died before me.
I called you my Queen, you were my Majesty
Don't put me through that pain,
I'd rather have bruddas laugh at me or blast at me
Than for you to be eaten by maggots whilst your body lays asleep.
I would rather be physically humiliated and have six feet
Than see you six feet under.

Undated 2011

Poem to the Merciful Loving Creator

Thank you God for blessing me with this natural talent
It comes so naturally; for others it's a challenge
I really think sometimes you control my eyes and they go blind
And my heart begins to find words to write about life,
If I should die tonight, I would not argue
Especially if I am destined to spend eternity with you.
I cannot see you but you are my best friend
This will continue to the very end, until the event of my demise.
I want to thank you for blessing me with a fantastic life
A beautiful family. Amazing friends and a genius mind.
Although I am misunderstood, an epitome of confusion
My love for you Jah, is not an illusion.
It is thanks to you I remain so hopeful
It is thanks to you why my life is so beautiful.

Undated 2011

Mystery

Our history is a mystery
But when it's being told it's illustrated with misery
We were kings and queens of the motherland
Until another man stole us from our mother's land
And look what he did, mocked, raped and disrespected
Slaves were kept then killed, whilst others selected

Undated 2011

My Mother

For nine months she carried me inside of her.
So for the rest of my days I shall walk beside her
Protect and respect her, bless her with the good news
As if I was a Messenger.
The message is; I love her for the rest of eternity
And I want to thank her for her maternity.
She nearly risked her life, so that I can live
So I will risk mine, so that I can give
Her, everything that her heart desires.
My heart burns with fire, an eternal flame
That erupts like a violent volcano because it will never love a woman
In the same way
As I love this one.
When she hugs me, she is warmer than the morning sun
So she comforts me before the day has begun.

Undated 2011

Letter to a Friend

It's a shame you got trapped in that system
It hurts my brain knowing you're caged in a cell in prison
But I hope you're feeling better, when you receive my letters
Showing you that none of the fond memories are missing.
Brother, I remember playing around in elementary
But it hurts my soul, was it meant to be
For you to be laying on bed in penitentiary?
But I stay positive, I own an optimistic mentality
But it's not easy when they take away your family.

No worries, because you are a dreamer.
A believer. An achiever, someone who wants to turn their life over
Onto a new page.
I look over my shoulder, and I'm missing a soldier
But I'm not filled with rage.
I'm filled with happiness; I see someone who wants to change
An intellectual who learnt from a silly mistake.

My brother, you're thinking positively
I didn't expect you to be
So believe me when I say respect is due
And I hope you know
The Most High is protecting you.
These words came from the heart
They're shining bright, a shining light in the dark.
Please remember, the memories we've shared
Will never depart.

3rd January 2012

Guilty Eyes

"I'm innocent"
Cold stares from twelve strangers. Ice slivered down his throat. Freezing.

She cried, each teardrop a foreign symbol for her pain.
She would never see him again; lonely nights were her new friends.
Why?

"I didn't do it, I'm innocent. Please"
Sweat.
His bottom lip bled, as his white daggers let go of their grip.
His eyes flashed left and right nervously, staring into oblivion.

She waited and waited for the answer and
She did not get the response she needed.

"I'm innocent".
She looked at him coldly, he looked at her.

With guilty eyes.

19th January 2012

In These Uncertain Times

Life as a young person seems to be getting harder
Sometimes I want to cry but I cover it up with laughter.
I think about my life and sometimes feel it is a disaster
Questioning society but I do not hear an answer.
Lord, what are my prospects?

Right now I'm forced to make tough decisions
Should I continue my revision?
Or spend an hour watching television?
So many fears and doubts as to what lies ahead,
Sometime I dream about my future, as I lay in bed.
Father, what are my options?

There are people dying,
Religious wars continue as blood pours on the concrete floor.
There are people fighting,
Aggravating the wounds of society which are already sore.
There are mothers crying,
Because they had to bury their sons due to knives and guns.
But I thank God, cos I'm still surviving.

In these uncertain times, who do I put my trust in?
Although I hear the dissonant sounds of police sirens,
And in this city of mine, I'm surrounded by violence.
I shall never suffer in silence, for you protect and guide me.
As exams come closer, as I grow older
I know you'll be there looking over my shoulder
For I am a child of God, a child of destiny
And your precious love has brought out the best in me!

9th October 2012

Still in Awe

I still look into her eyes and fall into the brown abyss
That they encapsulate.
Her flowing, glowing hair rolls down beyond her shoulders,
I am still in awe.
Her cheeks are sore, from flashing that fabulous seductive smile.
I probably still have feelings.
But I don't want to.

8th November 2012

Ubiquitous Individuals

Ubiquitous individuals; blurred by the need to conform within society.
Where are the heroes?
Bored with the gruelling regime of saving cursed men
Destined to a life of beautiful agony and ugly happiness.
Our lives are entwined and we find that we were never different.
Just homogeneous humans: hollow.
Sorrow. Pain. Anguish.
Banished thoughts of true freedom; we are constricted by the law.
Young men were conscripted for the War. Twice.

Lives wasted. Memories erased
Due to the monotony
Of the repetitive dichotomy:
Life and death.
Am I alike in my difference? NO!
Yes?

10th December 2012

Nan

Winter has passed; summer has finished.
She's gone
Aching hearts. Feelings diminished.
Dark zone.
Memories of what was once beautiful.
Pure.
Cancerous death. No cure.
My heart is sore.
She is out of pain, I am sure.

11th December 2012

Time 2

We find ourselves lost in coffins that are lost in
Time.
Time is a mental construction that causes so much detrimental destruction.
We are not dying and we are not living.
And we are not crying and we are not striving to survive;
We are just running out of time.
I never have enough time, procrastination is the biggest consumption
Of my precious minutes
I try to resist this; my frustration is the lack of resistance.
Time is continuous and it never stops.
It never stops but it may repeat.
It never stops but it may repeat.

Time to rest. Stress will compress and depress my mind into oblivion.
One second out of a million can determine the rest of my eternity.
My chest will eternally carry the organ
Which pumps the blood within me around me.
Time to see the blood which surrounds me.
Time to write to

My past, present and future.

Time 2 count the minutes that pass me by.
Time to count the lives that constantly die.
Do we only have one time to say goodbye and be free of
Time?

11th December 2012

Franklin's Rant

I've got something to tell.
I'm from a city where it's cool to kill,
But it's cruel to spill your emotions and express yourself.
I live in a place where I'm tired of running, I'm tumbling into situations
I don't want to be in
I'm filled with sins, so are my friends. I don't want to see them.
I hate what I've become but I love who I will be
But in reality will I ever get to live the dream?
It seems, we bleed for no reason. A different season;
A different brother, a different situation but the same outcome
Another mother forced to suffer.
I'm only thirteen but I'm old enough to get stabbed in my spleen and
Let it rupture.
My mother, a good hearted Christian, continues to warn me about the rapture.
I capture the images I see and put them on paper
And let my poetry speak.
My emotions seep through my pen, when I think about all the things
I'm going through.
Little girls are raised to be sex objects but
I'm still a virgin.
I'm emerging from the depths of society where all I see are killers
Pulling triggers and decreasing figures.
I have no friends, so I am alone, every evening
Due to the fact that my friends are not breathing, forever sleeping.
I'm a product of a cursed demon, who released semen
Into the womb of a beautiful woman who thought she was receiving
Love.
So he wonders why when I see him, I never believe him
When he says that he
Loves me.

I never want to be him.

But my environment may force me to repeat the mistakes of a generation

Repeated history.

Inherited misery.

So I look for father figures on these streets but all I see

Are murderers, drug dealers, fiends.

Nothing clean and nothing's good

Only bad happens in my neighbourhood, I should

Runaway and never return.

But a part of me will never learn and will always yearn

To go back and burn on the sharp edges of every curve and curb

To serve my life away. My life today is not mine.

I'm not lying, I belong to these streets.

Every time I try to leave I remember when Steve passed

That traffic light; I remember it clearly cos it was very bright

And then boom boom boom.

We prayed for Steve's soul that night, on the corner side.

That's all it is; another homicide.

Suicide is not my option

Nor is it a solution.

I thank my mother for not putting me up for adoption

And for her being resolute in

Disapproving abortion.

Life is hard and death is easy and they are never in proportion,

I pray to God and please believe me that I try so hard to be better.

Just remember that I do want things that are better.

But will they ever be and will they get to be?

Or am I set to be a failure?

An enigma shrouded in my misery, another victim to these streets.

Will I ever get to be Franklin or will I forget my name?

April 2014

Why Become a Poet?

I do not know what compelled me to want to be a poet.
I know they won't name any buildings after me and surely I will
Not
Be remembered for my innermost feelings and nuanced thoughts.
I assume that I am just another sentimental, temperamental individual
Searching for that something that stops my solitude.
Yet I cannot soothe the soul of this tortured man.
Limited to boundless opportunities.

What compelled me to be a poet is the fact that I want to be.

20th October 2014

The Prettiest Days

The prettiest days were once all that Aphrodite intended them to be:
We were free, young and most importantly in love.
Encapsulated in love's capsule; it hid us from hideous.
Delirious, serious feelings healed our loneliness
Stars aligned as our bodies entwined to produce a sinful synergy
God was envious of not creating.
Infallible was our time together as imperfections evaded
There was no deliberating and debating:
I loved you and I was proud to be part of life
That highlighted the failings of mine.

"So much of life is wasted on loneliness. I'm sweeter than your solitude"
Simple sentiments left me confused.
I was not aware how amazing it could be to bask
In the atmosphere of love and affection.
You were the beginning and now the end of my happiness,
I gallivant in the midst of depression's direction.
I learnt too late.
You were wrong; too much of life is wasted for those who wait.
I hate time and patience is a virtue that I do not want to possess.
Declarations, exclamations of one's feelings I will never again profess.

As time escaped us so did your feelings of infatuation.
Suddenly
I returned to a place you made me regret ever coming from.
Music is bland and bleak regardless of intentions of beauty
For the girl who I fell in love with and made this heart syncopate
Has left for reasons unexplained and this dying organ is one that will
Never be played again.

9th November 2014

The Higher Spirits

Sometimes I get in touch with the higher spirits and talk to my forefathers
We reminisce on times before fathers walked away from the seeds
They planted in the fertile land of Nubian Queens.
They told me that the rain drops we know as precipitation
Were just products of perspiration
From the angels dancing.
Nations were not formed just by primordial bonds
But a common destiny.

9th November 2014

You Will Never Understand

You equate your penis with weapons of power and mass destruction
Like a Beretta in the hand
Of a soldier intent on doing harm; emotions scarred from the corruption
That is happening inside the heart of a creature from a distant land.
You see sex as an activity where you enter and trespass private gardens
Where you plant and sow seeds in the fertile lands of womanhood
Only to disregard the attentive nurture needed for nature to truly run its course.
Of course
You will never understand
For this is for the misogynists, all men in the world who abuse women's
Wombs in search for that maternal connection
Or simply to heal internal wounds.

Or are all the men in the world who abuse women's wombs in search of
Their maternal connection
Divine feminine womb energy that you seek.

11th November 2014

Intruder

As I run away from the insecurities I try to ignore;
Fleeing fleeting feelings,
She writes words that exude pain
Yet welcome memories of acceptance.
Nostalgia.

Secret sorrows that we choose not to share,
We all have them yet there comes a time where all is revealed.
Closure is at times better than a solution.
She confided in a stranger who would not judge.

His touch, scent and eyes still haunt her.
Innocence can be recaptured yet it'll never be the same.
He was caught up in the rapture of lust.

22nd November 2014

Black Phoenix

Greatness never leaves.
It is the energy that transfers from one being to another
Just like traditions continue yet evolve;
We used to worship the Sun and now we worship the Son.
Time is a cycle that man will never understand completely.
As I run towards the past I stare at memories of my future;
I walk with the same spirit of Malcom
Educating young brothers who sell drugs
The same colour and consistency as talcum
Powder.
Power is inherent
As I consistently aim to achieve beyond your expectations:
I write with the vigour of a thousand Africans picking cotton.
I am a slave to the talent my master has given me.
I am blessed because Martin has forgiven me
In my dreams.
I have foreseen events that constitute a time where we are no longer
In a desolate place.
Conversations with Kinte and Kuti
About how the motherland continues to be raped
Leave the arteries of this dying African heart in disarray.
But there is a beacon of hope
Echoed by the words of Steve Biko:
Black is beautiful.
But sometimes beauty is not recognised
Even by those who possess it.

Garvey galvanised the mind of many;
Stimulating black brothers and sisters
To acknowledge their worth

Even through stressful times
For pressure makes diamonds.
We are those diamonds.
But our heroes and leaders were killed
In the same cruelty
Reminiscent to the gallons of blood spilled amongst the wooden
Floors that held us captive.
Captivate your own minds, I say
The teachings of those before you lead to a future better than now.

Sister, let no man diminish your worth!
Use the life of Maya to inspire
Yourselves to create women who do not burn or singe from
The harshness of life's fire
But are reborn.

Let Angela remind you that although society cannot handle the
Flame that keeps your passion burning
You are not aggressive, obsessive, possessive
Just
Expressive.
I urge you to never forget this:
The warmth of your hands cultivate cultures sculptors could never create.

The everlasting presence of past figures caress your future.
The fingers clasp onto the very essence of positivity
But also guide you to a better now.
I say do not burn the history that breeds you;
Never forget where you came from.
The journey is not over
It is a long walk to freedom.

25th November 2014

They Use the Drumbeat

They use the drumbeat to capture the rhythmic rituals of my ancestors
But the syncopation of my heartbeat is more than enough
To recreate the sensation of those slaves who led the Haitian Revolution.
Where are my indemnities?
We know the history and what caused my father's land
To be in the position it is today
We are portrayed as poor and helpless...

13th December 2014

Potent Silence

They just don't understand and that's why my silence is potent
It saves the older generation from disappointment.
Dreams are not meant to be discarded
They are regarded as fragile and delicate
And therefore they should be guarded.
As an artist I don't just rhyme words that play with the hearts chords
I illustrate lucid, fluid images that would force others to think I hallucinate.
I am a person who follows their passion,
Fruits of my labour will never perish
And will plant seeds that will flourish and I will surely cherish.
I told my mother with all due respect she does the things that she can
I do the things that I can't.
Society expects me to conform to their limitations
Forgetting that...

31st December 2014.

More Than Poetry

We are only free prisoners trapped in life's deadly chains
Belonging is an arbitrary paradox: providing social cohesion yet ostracising
Those they can no longer understand.
All I see is division across this land as I'm armed with the greatest
Instrument in my hand.
This pen is an extension of me as it declares that
This is more than a poem.
This is the writing of a young boy sitting in his public library that
The government plans to demolish.
A poem that witnesses hopeless eyes being penetrated by corrosive tears
That coerce and blackmail a black male to bare the cries of his ancestors
Due to an ignorant teacher that said slavery should never have been abolished.
This poem is honest
For it is the utterances of single mothers who are still in love with
Men that neglect
The possibility of fathering a child after their penises are erect.
Political tirades tarnish the thoughts of many;
Magnifying mantras that manipulate mankind
To hate.
The kindness of man only seems to last
When one seems to pass
The test of normality.
Individuality is a celebrated failure.

I'll say it again if I have to:
This is more than poetry
This is the documentation of my brother selling drugs of the highest
Potency in exchange for currency.

We currently live in a society dictated by capitalism
And capital isn't everyone's forte.
I shudder when I reminisce about the things I used to do for pay.
I see young brothers and sisters who need forgiveness as well as assistance
As today they struggle to make a brighter tomorrow.
University fees will leave my mother's pockets hollow
As I aim to follow my dreams
And yet my friend whose mind is greater than mine
Is tormented by the sorrow that encases her ambition
As she tries to find another way to succeed.
These are words of life acknowledging the times we are dying in.

This is spoken word announcing words that were left unspoken;
The silent screams of the heartbroken:
An emblem of hope for those that were left hopeless
Whilst hoping for better days
Please use your time wisely as it tries to suffocate itself slowly
And let your beauty manifest and cascade onto a society filled with social ills
As it seems to kill
Creativity.
Are you wrong to conform to a society you help create
But don't want to belong to?
For too long, we have been blind to our own greatness;
The residue of fallen stars
That helped to form this earth
Formed you. You were born to
Not belong but be entwined with one another.
So why continue to suffer?

Which one of you will live to be the change that you want to see?
You already possess the key to unlock these chains
But yet most of you will allow the cycle of conformity to continue.
Death is inevitable. You are afraid to live.
You are afraid to give and you are afraid to lift yourselves
To the position most natural according to your being
Are you afraid of freedom?

You are, only, free prisoners trapped in life's deadly chains.
You do belong.

Undated 2014

Today

Today is the oldest we are and the youngest we will ever be.
Embrace the fact that you are ever changing.
Never static nor constant
For the essence of your being was and forever shall be malleable;
Shaped by the situations you do not want to face.

Time can only restrict the woman who adheres to its existence.
Do not envy the wind for it is duplicitous and haunted.
Travelling from coast to coast,
Soothing scorched skin as it carries summer's breeze,
Forcing you to forget that it can uproot
Take pride

9th January 2015

The Role of the Poet

Observing the world from a safe distance
I write
Thoughts that my mother would be astounded by for she doesn't understand
The melancholy that strokes the arteries of this heart.
My blood soaks the page, each word written serves a purpose
Nothing is by accident; fate only exists in the minds of who believe it.
In the midst of silence
Echoes of villagers burning from the hands of mad men
From a distant land enter the room
And penetrate the ear drums that try to ignore it.
I cry tears that they never had the chance to,
I still feel the faintest breeze that caress and tease the hairs of my skin
I still feel the direct injustice that forces me to empathise
With men and women, I will never know.
I understand.

I am that, I am; I write poems that heal the hearts of many
Yet cannot soothe the soul of this tortured man.

1st February 2015

I am

And it continues,
Forever lamenting,
Lurking,
Lying in the darkness that the light evades.
I am the thing death cannot solicit nor sleep can waver
Yet my happiness is subdued.
I bare my soul to strangers as I am not comfortable enough to express
My sorrows to my friends.
I do not want to burden you with my burdens.
I am nobody. I am irrelevant.
You will not know who I am
For you will not take the time to decipher the writing
That depicts the unravelling of a human being, being human.
This is not a display of the supine or fragile nature to a creature seeking pity
Nor is it the description of the perils and plights of what happens within my city.
This is the language of despair that is enunciated by a man trying to question
Why his sweetest days are sour?
I want to cherish every last moment of joy yet I cannot
For the satisfaction ceases to exist in my world of bleak fulfilment.
I already know that I have this problem.
I beg you
Please refrain from making it more obvious
To a man who looks vacantly into the mirror's reflection
And scrutinises every feature that is etched on this face of sin.
They say the life unexamined is a life not worth living;
Never shall I be the physical embodiment of such a statement.
Whilst I live in hope, I hope to live.

What do you do when the very thing you seek eludes you?
Every effort to capture the joy
That hopes to make your life worthwhile is tarnished,
It withers away from the scalding furnace that your passion exudes
As it is not yet pleased.
What purpose do I have when the thing that makes me feel
Is the same thing that makes me fall?
Fall into the abyss of solitude and immerse myself in the presence
Of weeping silence.
I do not know how to feel
When I tell my lover that she makes me smile with my heart?
Every time that we are apart
I am overcome with the same loneliness that forces the wolves to howl
As they know they can never make love with the moon.
Yes, I love her and I am proud to be part of a life
That highlights the failings of mine
But how true is my love if she will never fill the void that misery creates?
I do feel guilt every time self-centred notions enter this mind
As I know that young children are poisoned by the water they pray for.
However, just like the adolescence of the man you see in front of you,
My empathy vanishes quicker than I can recall.

Who and what am I?
What kind of man am I
When I long to go back to the comfort of my mother's womb?
I am the figment of your imagination that you do not utilise.
I am merely a part of the atmosphere
You do not acknowledge but know is there.
A perpetual aura.

The duplicitous wind, carrying secrets of a past it longs to forget,
As it searches for its birthplace but has nowhere to die.
Yes, I am the thing that death cannot solicit nor sleep can waver
Yet sadness, from an unfulfilled passion, still tortures me.

So therefore I am nobody. I am that thing.

16th February 2015

Breaking News

Stephen Wallace.
Black male.
22 years old.
Shot three times in the torso.
London
He died at 6.45pm

You will hear and read articles, reports and accounts
Of the life of this criminal.
But you will never know his wants and aspirations, fears and tribulations.
You will not know the person, only the individual.
He was not the first to die and he will surely not be the last.
Bubbling and brewing, these events will erupt from the cauldron
That we call the past.
You will forget his name. You WILL forget his name.
Another youth slain.

A wanderer stuck in the land that politicians will never roam.
A traveller trapped in an area where the youth will never possess
Property to call their own.
A product of an environment where the climate will never change,
It will never change
You will forget his name; you will forget his names.

30th January 2015

S.O.S: Scared Of Safety

Why do they want to disgrace me? Do they hate me?
They stop and search me, supposedly,
For my own safety and the safety of others.
I am not complaining alone because they search my brothers.
I try not to be like my friends so I don't carry a knife
But what I do carry inside is foolish pride which longs for vengeance.
However, if I retaliate with hate they can take my life away
Or give me a prison sentence.
I want to strike.
Revenge plagues my mind.
The only thing that stops me
Is the fact that, freedom is so hard to find
When it seems to hide, as you try to stay alive behind prison walls.
A couple brothers are not here in attendance
On this Earth and that hurts.
So for what it's worth we pray for dead soldiers to show remembrance.

I have seen it before, what is happening isn't new and this is true;
My mother has shown me the effects that have left our communities sore.
I'm sure police brutality knows no limits. I fear the possibilities
They could put me in a hearse, my mother crying at my funeral for she is cursed,
Forever hurting as she carries the burden of outliving her only son.
How many people have been crippled with disabilities?
Due to police overstepping their responsibilities?
I fear it's more than one!
We will never — we will never know the true answer.
No wonder why I seem so miserable, I seldom smile,
I see them stroll and every time I see them
The sense of freedom goes.

Lines can be blurred when agendas are just meaningless words.

The only difference between the police and criminals is the matter of legitimacy

And although I am afraid of what they both can do,

I know that only a certain few can get away with murder.

I have seen many victims of society trapped in coffins that get forgotten by time

Only because they were killed by those who are meant to instil order.

I can only murmur these thoughts of mine; I will never state my frustration

As they truly won't listen to a child of my age filled with rage.

My fear has taught me,

Irrespective of the stereotypical view

Gangsters can be legal too.

I have no trust in those that are meant to serve and protect!

I hate them with a passion that I will surely regret,

For there will be a time, very soon

Where I will depend on them;

On these streets there are liars, cheats and heartless thieves

And anything can happen.

Anything can happen and I see death around the corner,

I am ready to call the coroner

But

I feel guilty before I have even called their line.

To them I am a delinquent, a criminal before I have committed any crime.

I was born a statistic and I was born a threat

The multiple murders over the years do not help to defeat this stereotype

But they do not care.

We fight and die over land we do not own; strangers in our own home.

We make their jobs easier by making our lives harder.

So please tell me why would they save someone who is intent on dying?

April 2015

I Will Kiss You

I will kiss you
In the winter of your lifetime
So that you feel the warmth,
Calming yet rhapsodic,
Of lips that long to please yours.

I will protect you although life's weapons are apparent
And death is daunting,
They cannot impair the spirit of a man
Who I strengthened

I will make you smile
Even when your jaw is clenched
And your heart is laden with bitterness.

Slowly, surely
You will return
In the meantime,

I will remain
Slowly surely.

23rd May 2015

I Should Say Sorry Momma

I know you might feel pain from knowing that your son
Wants to drop out of University
It isn't for me.
Your son was meant to shine universally
To warm the people, warn the people
About the detriment of harbouring pain and evil
I cannot be restricted or compromised to one degree.
Writing essays about politics
I will be talking about the BS that we see in society.
This leaves me disheartened, wondering if I'll ever be a
Virtuous contributor to my community.
Aspirations of taking vacations to California whilst I reside in Soledad
I guess my loneliness is solely because of my dad
Because I'm the son of a man who worships the Son of man
But never taught his son how to be a man.
So there I was and here I am
Alone and confused
But I can't complain, we all have our own struggles.
I remember conversations with a friend who was feeling hopeless
As he reminisced over memories of when he was homeless
Collecting pennies to make a pound just to buy four wings and chips
He said "Alex you don't know what hope is!"
I've been depressed since I left the womb, I don't know where my soul is.

I saw things you wouldn't want your boy to see, momma.
Cocaine
Coke cans used as ash trays
I met a beautiful girl named Mary.

Mary wanna have fun
But her life of opulence has decadent effects.
She asked me what keeps me alive
And I said it's you, Momma
You taught me that even when I'm poor, I can still be rich in spirit
But all she seems to do is drink richer spirits
Rum, vodka and absinthe
I run form the vulgar yet I sink into an abyss
That forces me to succumb to solitude.
And I miss my childhood, Momma.

And if I do graduate
It will be with a degree that is worth more than a third
But it will burn just the same.
These will be the three best years of loneliness
Writing political essays about Thomas
Life is nasty, brutish and short: Pain

31st May 2015

I Doubt

I know she doesn't love me anymore.
I doubt
I don't think she remembers
The laughter, the wine, the photos
Happiness.
Our friendship vanished

13th July 2015

Tainted Beauty

Loose insecurities.
Lose insecurities!
The surety
Of life's pressures is evident
In the media's reflections
Of what
Is beautiful and relevant.
Who are they to decide what beauty is?
Toddlers, children, young people
Will grow
Inevitably
But will they know
Their worth
Indefinitely?

Social structures are very prevalent.
We are the persistent assailant
Of our confidence.
Compliments are not substantial;
Merely condiments
That temporarily carry
The unsatisfactory taste of disappointment
That has ruined the tongues of those deprived of self-assurance.

We now portray beauty in an ugly fashion.

13th July 2015

Will I Ever Make It?

Will I ever make it?
This question haunts me
But I gotta continue
Cos where I'm from greatness isn't promised.
This lonely journey is painful
But I gotta stay focused.
I won't give up.
I run from the past
As I chase my destiny.

Still I move.
I breathe.
Heavily.
I run
Closer,
Harder,
Faster
Towards my dreams.
This passion is burning inside of me.
I want more from my life.
I won't give up.

Will I ever make it?
I have to.

29th August 2015

One Day

I pray that your children will not feel uncomfortable in places that they belong.
I pray they find a home
One where they feel comfortable, enough to explore and roam.
I study and reside in a university, an institution of excellence
In the eyes of wider society and although
I never swum in the shallow pools of satiety
I am proud of where I came from. Yes, I am proud of where I came from.
The tall estates stood slanted, dilapidated in need of decoration
And in some ways they reflect the image of the young people who lived within
These trappings of relative poverty.
These were the fortresses of misfortune where young soldiers fought over
Issues they cannot remember only to be killed and forgotten.
This mist of doom will never leave, I will always grieve
Because those young men never knew they were kings.
So I left to new pastures and aspired to achieve the green that will leave
The impoverished envious and myself wealthy.
I found myself in a university where my endeavours were diminished
By the comments of ignorance that told me I should feel
Privileged, lucky and blessed
To be in an institution that is better than the rest.
How am I to feel when critical thinking forces me to know what they truly mean?
I am not lucky; I am not blessed: I deserve this!
I left an area where stagnant nomads feel deserted
Where politicians never visit or never heard of the people who voted for them
To represent us only for them to neglect and resent us.
I said words that were expletives and my mother said were too explicit
Because of the frustration and fatigue of those sleepless nights

3rd December 2015

Crippled

Social mash — lack of purpose
The problem does not go away
My friendships are disintegrating
Paralysing, it's crippling
Prisoner to my mind;
I don't even want to finish this life sentence
Stigma!!!

Undated 2015

Dear Diary

I'm a fucking mess!
I am thinking of murdering myself,
Taking the life my mother so faithfully prays for.
I don't want to live anymore.
I feel like a prisoner who cannot endure this life sentence.
Days seem to blur into one another
As my existence is futile and decayed.
There has been a diminution in my character, as I no longer find
Enjoyment from the things that used to bring my life meaning.
I cannot bear to witness the sin etched on this black face
So I refuse to look in the mirror.
They remain oblivious to my suffering,
I wonder if they see the signs?
My appetite left as quickly as my childhood,
I'm vanishing; my fragile bones are no longer protected by the skin and flesh
That used to clothe them.
Somebody gouge out these eyes from their socket
These glassy marbles are stained windows to a murky soul
And what use are they if I cannot cry?

I miss happiness
Even though I don't remember what she feels like.
Pleasure seems so distant
As my sweetest days are sour.
My life is a cauldron of repressed anger and despair.
So I tend to avoid social events, unless I have to
Conversations were such a delight but now they are merely transactions
I have to go through.
My closest friends are strangers to me.
I feel so lonely amongst them.
But how are they to know?

As I mask my feelings incredibly.
I continue to make them smile, laugh rapturously
But when I go home I am researching how to die quietly and quickly.

My thoughts are like rats scurrying
Amongst the sewage of a wasted mind.
My prayers are now corrupt as I feel that God has forsaken me.
No one understands — I wish they knew.
I wish they heard the weeping silence
I wish they called for help so they could section me,
Encase me in a strait jacket,
Forcing my languid arms to wrap around my frail torso, ever so tightly
Maybe that's the closest I'll ever get
To self-love. A hug

My insecurities cripple me but depression paralyses my spirit.
This weakness sickens me.
Perplexed — I question where it came from
All I know is that I am drowning in boiling water,
Screaming internally, writhing in pain
Watching beautiful people play
Happily, on the shore.

I feel shame every time I try to reach acceptance.
So much stigma
Their comments and judgements
Are like vultures ripping into the carcass that I currently reside in.
I don't want to open up just to shut down.
Can I be cured or am I doomed?
What kind of man am I, when
I long to go back to my mother's womb?

Undated 2015

Rise Again

My brothers and sisters
I urge you to look, please look around
And stare at what surrounds you.
Question whether these moments, ephemeral and ethereal,
Are the dreams of our ancestors?
The oaths of our leaders.
Is this... it?
Is this it?

If we use slavery as our starting point
Then anything thereafter will be seen as progress.
Be insatiable!
May the illusion of freedom,
The misconception of paradise
Never beguile you.
Yes, our history precedes us,
We have a common lineage
But don't you know
That we have a shared destiny.

Please forgive me.
The dexterity of my lyricism,
The depth of these words
Cannot conjure up pictures of paradise
Nor do they mean to conceal
The struggle that is liberation.
I wish my tongue was swift
With the language of inspiration
But it is as heavy as the
Sea of despair that nearly
Drowned Nkrumah.

Yet, still I persist
To implore
You to move forward,
Towards your destination.

March on!
Brothers and sisters,
She will rise up again.
Grab your sword, grab your rod, grab your pen
Whatever your talent, use it
For that is the only way
She will overcome her reputation of destitution.
Soon, they will learn
That they can never pillage
Our village, our land, our sanctum.
They fear our unity.
She begs for her children
To stand in solidarity.
She begs and pleads.
I echo the words of Ghana's famous son
"We are going to demonstrate to the world.
To other nations, that we are prepared
To lay our foundation,
Our own African personality.
Our independence is meaningless
Unless it is linked with the total
Liberation of Africa."

She will rise again.
You decide, brothers and sisters
When!

Undated 2015

I Am Love

I was writing poetry before the womb,
I was talking to God before he created the stars and the moon,
I was climbing clouds
Catching comets,
Callously as my calluses could not burn,
As I clasped, into the corners of the sun.

I was a father to sons who were never mine,
I was a teacher,
Before the Moors brought culture to Europe,
I was alive before time was recognised as time.

I was talking to the spirits of your forefather's ancestors
As we plotted plans that would prevent our enslavement,
I was a mystery before the people of Africa
Lost their history.

I was there

But unfortunately the bullets missed me
I could have saved the innocent victims of police brutality.
Now misery,
Misery is all that I see.

I was the ancient remedy
That would reverse
The effects of dysentery
Or any disease.

I was known,
Yet I was not vague,
I was creation.
I was the amalgamation,
The culmination of the nation.

I was before,
Before you treated your women like common whores
And sex was treated like a game
For men to keep a tally
To see the score.

Before territories saw pterodactyls, terrorise beautiful skies.
I was fruit, before it got revolutionised.
I was the language,
I was the language that bound the world together
Before it became globalised.

I was truth,
Set free and liberated.
I was never civilised.
I was civilisation.
I was emancipation,
I was freedom.

I was the fondest memories,
Collections of stories
That soothed your soul
As you lost control,
As euphoria would overcome you.

I was dance,
I was song,
I was music,
I was the message on the land that gave meaning to cupid.
I was lucid.
I was the laughter,
The laughter of the school children
Carefree and naïve
Before they realised they could
Never afford to pay the university tuition fees.

I was the weakness you feel when you get lost
Into her eyes and bend down on one knee,
For your happiness is now embodied,
To your mother's cries when she realised
That she was no longer living for herself.

I was selfless.
There for you when you felt helpless
I was the reason you smiled,
I flowed freely like the river Nile,
I was

Omnipotent, solely potent
I was the reason,
I was the reason for the inception of mystical potions,
Lotions, notions, oceans,
Could not compare with the depth of my being.

I was, I was freeing
You from the chains of hatred,
I was sacred,
I was ancient,
Yet renewed constantly,
I was never tainted,
No matter what they tell you,
Because I can never be manipulated in my purest form.

You see I am the thing that will survive your very existence,
Commemorating your life with passion and persistence,
I am the thing that makes you feel,
And the thing that makes you fall,
I am the thing that conquers all.

I was relevant;

I AM
I AM LOVE
I AM LOVE

January 2016

Malcom's Poem; Feb 21

Made us use our most powerful weapon: our mind
This great and gentle man reminded us of our humanity
That it is never too late to reinvent oneself
He was the black phoenix
A nation is cemented not by the land it occupies but by the stories that it tells
And silences — to justify its existence
Unimpeachable integrity
His influence lives on, rings
How does a former drug dealer become a demigod?
How can an ex-convict be labelled a demagogue?
How can one man, within 39 years of existence
Embody and symbolise black America
How are you successful if you feel unfulfilled?
You cannot legislate goodwill
Flashes of brilliance whenever he opened his mouth to express
Who is willing to change the miserable condition that exists on the Earth?

Our distinguished guests, brothers and sisters
Our friends and our enemies, everybody is here
To witness the extolling of our black prince, brother Malcolm.
I am honoured to stand here in front of you
And offer to you a contributory note about a man I wish I hugged several times.
These words are like the tears my father never shed in front of me;
Visceral and impassioned
Embodying a vulnerability, I seldom show.
Please forgive my sentimentality
But I have to honour this man, of unimpeachable integrity,
By any means necessary.

I prayed that my new year's resolutions would be revolutions
So I could be a better man.
I found Malcolm at a time where I was disillusioned
Lost and entangled by the vicious vines
That only a concrete jungle can produce.
The lion cubs found pleasure playing in cages
And then grew up killing one another just to survive.
I tried to walk with the spirit of Malcolm
Educating young brothers who sold drugs
The same colour and consistency
As talcum powder.
Power is inherent
But I wasn't to know until I came across his book
I saw the parallels.
I saw the traits that made this black phoenix
So relatable
What made Malcolm so great was his accessibility to all
The thug, the criminal, drug addict, the intellectual,
Revolutionary and scholar.
I saw his humanity through the flaws he refused to conceal.

He asked the question that still haunts us
"Who taught you how to hate yourself?"
Berate yourself, negate your wealth
Disavow the essence of your being and emancipate yourself.
It was brother Malcom.
Colonialism still pervades and of course it still persists,
The remnants of slavery are still alive and true and racism still exists.
Magnificence of melanin

Our democracy is hypocrisy

They told me it stood for power to the people

But all I see is powder in my people

I pray that I am a cancer to this evil

That plagues this land.

Most likely I will die just like Malcom

The authorities and my own brothers of this nation will conspire to kill me

Either due to fear or jealousy.

I'm calling for action, I need to see a drastic change

I'm echoing the thoughts of my namesake

As I enunciate the need for a social revolution

We can change this society

15th February 2016

Alternative Franklin's Rant

I've got something to tell.
I'm from a city where it's cool to kill,
But it's cruel to spill your emotions and express yourself.
I live in a place where I'm tired of running, I'm tumbling into situations
I don't want to be in
I'm filled with sins, so are my friends. I don't want to see them.
I hate who I am but I love who I will be
But in reality will I ever get to live the dream?
It seems, we bleed for no reason. A different season;
A different brother, a different situation but the same outcome
Another mother forced to suffer.
I'm only sixteen but I'm old enough to get stabbed in my spleen and
Let it rupture.
My mother, a good hearted Christian, continues to warn me about the rapture.
I capture the images I see and put them on paper
And let my poetry speak.
My emotions seep through my pen, when I think about all the things
I'm going through.
Little girls are raised to be sex objects but
I'm still a virgin.
I'm emerging from the depths of society where all I see are killers
Pulling triggers and decreasing figures.
I have no friends, so I am alone, every evening
Due to the fact that my friends are not breathing, forever sleeping.
I'm a product of a cursed demon, who released semen
Into the womb of a beautiful woman who thought she was receiving
Love.
So he wonders why when I see him, I never believe him
When he says that he
Loves me.

I never want to be him.

But my environment may force me to repeat the mistakes of a generation

Repeated history.

Inherited misery.

So I look for father figures on these streets but all I see

Are murderers, drug dealers, fiends.

Nothing clean and nothing's good

Only bad happens in my neighbourhood, I should

Run away and never return.

But a part of me will never learn and will always yearn

To go back and burn on the sharp edges of every curve and curb

To serve my life away. My life today ain't mine.

I ain't lying, I belong to these streets.

Every time I try to leave I remember when Steve passed that traffic light;

I remember it clearly cos it was so bright

And then boom boom boom.

We prayed for Steve's soul that night, on the corner side.

That's all it is; another homicide.

Suicide has never been an option nor is it a solution.

I thank my mother for not putting me up for adoption

And for her being resolute in

Disapproving abortion.

Life is hard and death is easy and they are never in proportion,

I pray to God and please believe me that I try so hard to be better.

Just remember that I do want things that are better.

But will they ever be and will they get to be?

Or am I set to be a failure?

An enigma shrouded in my misery, another victim to these streets.

Will I ever get to be Franklin or will I forget my name?

28th February 2016

Peace of Mind! The Last Poem

I have witnessed the fragility of life!
I have seen it ebb away.
I have seen the plights and perils of urban decay;
Where young boys became misguided entrepreneurs
Leading a life of crime in their prime
Whilst young sisters and their bodies
Became sexualised before they even have had their period on time.
I thought I had seen it all but
To the might of God, I was blind.
Although I was raised in the church
I left to search for something that
I thought would soothe the suffering of my soul,
Not understanding that Christ was and is
The panacea for my woes
And was
The only thing that could have ever made me whole.

Please forgive the lack of dexterity in my lyricism
But this is not a poem!
This is probably the closest I will ever get to ministry
So this is my sermon with hopes for tomorrow.
I still pray for my friends who
Drown their sorrows in the bottom of the bottle.
Right now, I am rich in spirit
Whilst they drink the richest spirits.
I am living, they are livid.
I have finally accepted my Father's love.

Therefore, who am I to complain?
Even with a lesion, a possible tumour on my brain?
There are children being poisoned by the water that they pray for!
I am thankful — this whole experience was the impetus I needed
That has allowed me to pray more!
I have conversations with Christ,
They have been sacred and sincere,
I have no fear.
For three weeks ago I was in a coma
And now I am here
Littering the stage with pieces of my psyche.
Please forgive me! I wrote these words in less than 10 minutes
With a stick that was running out of ink
But happened to capture my blood and allow it to grace this page.
I have a lot on my brain
But I thank the Father for giving me peace of mind,
Before the doctors take a piece of mine.
I have been still in His presence
And accepted the gift of faith.
I have humbled myself and given Him my trust
For Roman's 8:18 says
"For I consider that our present sufferings are not worth comparing
With the glory that will be revealed in us"

No, I am not a poet and
This is not a poem.
I am simply a man who has
Experienced and encountered love
And I refuse to be selfish with this blessing.
These are merely words that fail to offer the Lord, my God
The glory and honour that He truly deserves!

9th April 2016

In loving memory
of Alexander "King" Paul

Lightning Source UK Ltd.
Milton Keynes UK
UKHW02f0450260518
323244UK00002B/3/P